One Foot in the Joy

Living & loving through cancer

One Foot in the Joy

Living & loving through cancer

Suzy Goodsell

Goodsell Graphics, 2011
Elk River, MN

An earlier edition of this book was published under the title *One Foot in the Joy, Living & loving through cancer, The first year.*

One Foot in the Joy
Living & loving through cancer

First printing, October 2009
Second printing & revision, October 2011

Copyright © Suzanne C. Goodsell, 2009, 2011
All rights reserved

ISBN 978-0-9839940-0-8

Printed in the United States of America

Cover design by Suzanne Kienietz
Cover photography by Dan Routhe
Edited by Judy Hynes

GOODSELL GRAPHICS
Elk River, MN 55330

These pages are dedicated to:

God, my savior, friend and healer, who gave me the gift to lay down the words.

My husband, Dan, who walked through these pages with me.

My children Katlynn, Elisa, Matt and Seth, who also share the journey.

My parents, Ted and Nancy, who have loved me from the beginning, and sister, Lori, who shares my creative heart with paintbrushes rather than words.

Foreword

I started this story in an uncomfortable place: Not knowing how the story ends.
I love tidy-ending books and happy-ending movies. I don't even mind a painful route as long as I'm assured of a good outcome.

But I'm not.

There's no way I can begin this journey with any capacity to know where it will take me.

So in order to finally begin putting these words together, I had to let go of that expectation. I had to care more about finding joy along the way than knowing the last line.

I'm now four years from my original diagnosis. I still have active cancer, but I'm still here.

None of us knows what the future holds, but there are moments when we realize how important it is to pay attention to the precious moments we find in each day.

What I've learned is that life isn't a series of consecutive ups and downs. There is always joy. There is always challenge.
And the two always exist at the same time.

When I came to that place, I knew I could begin.

Soon after my diagnosis and surgery, I started blogging as a way to give my friends and family members my health updates.

For me, it became more. It was my way of documenting the journey I had found myself on.

These words are not just about cancer or serious illness, but about how each of us lives our life, every day. It's about how we weave life's worries, difficulties and crises into the ordinary kitchen clean-ups and commutes.

So, welcome to my story.

Prologue

Life had been hectic after a divorce that began four years prior to my cancer diagnosis. After 17 years of marriage, I found myself 40 years old, single and with full custody of three children who were then aged 5, 7 and 9. Within five years, I'd returned to full-time work, sorted through my daughter's newly diagnosed diabetes, found myself in a new relationship, and then remarried to a great guy, Dan.

During this time, I'd been noticing a sort of "dust in my throat" feeling and had a very minor cough. I brought it up during a couple of regular doctor visits. One physician's assistant thought it might be acid reflux and suggested taking a double dose of antacids every day for a month. Later, another medical professional, during my annual appointment, suggested I try an inhaler to see if the cough was related to asthma.

It wasn't. In fact, it was something altogether different. On Nov. 5, 2007, I wrote in my personal journal:

"I had a meeting today. Oh my gosh, I must be losing it! I was in a conference room filled with half a dozen staff members from a different department who were asking for my input about how best to get information out to employees. Because I was filling in for my boss who was traveling, I was the only representative from my communications team.

"At first it was easy – I just listened. But once they started asking me for feedback, I realized I was having trouble verbalizing my thoughts. I could see the words in my head, but just couldn't wrap my mind around them to spit them out. I felt like a lunatic. Several times, I'd start talking and then stop mid-stream. Everyone would look at me, and then someone would try to finish my sentence for me.

"What's wrong with me?"

Panicked, I cancelled my meetings and tried not to answer my phone. This was of great concern because I earn a living as a writer and manager in corporate communications. I could still write stories for our employee home page and email, but it took longer than usual.

At home, the kids definitely noticed that something was up. I wrote:

> *"This is crazy. I went downstairs to try to talk to my daughter, Katlynn, and I sat there in silence. I'd say a couple of words and then stop. Later, I tried again and she asked me, 'Mom, are you going to do that slow talking thing again?'"*

After another week of similar symptoms, my boss returned to the office. She'd called me a few times while she had been gone, but I'd had a hard time talking. I could agree with her, and say, "Yeah" and "Uh-huh," but I wasn't initiating conversation at all.

When she leaned over my work cube wall and asked me how I was, I said, "OK." Then she asked, "Are you and I OK?" Frustrated, I said that we were fine, but that I just couldn't complete a whole sentence. We laughed about being 40-something and a little forgetful. But later she suggested I make an appointment at the on-site health clinic, just to check things out.

When I went to the appointment the following day, I brought with me a list of symptoms that I'd written out ahead of time because I wasn't sure I'd be able to articulate what was wrong.

I began reading my symptom list. After only a few sentences, the physician's assistant stopped me.

"Suzy, this isn't normal for you."

I paused and looked at him, feeling like he had just stated the obvious, but was suddenly concerned about what could possibly be wrong.

"Can you take tomorrow off and have someone drive you to see a neurologist?"

In my mind, I thought, "What's a neurologist?" But I told him that I could.

The next day, Dan (who I was dating at the time and would eventually marry) drove me to the neurology appointment. That appointment led to getting a brain MRI that night at 10 p.m. and then a follow-up with Dr. R the next day.

Initially, the results seemed positive. He told me that he had suspected that I might have had a minor stroke, but I didn't.

I breathed a short-lived sigh of relief.

"You didn't have a stroke, Suzy. The problem is tumor related."

He told me I had a walnut-sized tumor located outside of my left frontal lobe. Dan immediately began asking questions about the type of tumor, but I was numb. He said that it had probably been there for nearly a year, and for whatever reason, it had hemorrhaged or just bumped against my verbal center.

Dr. R ordered two tests, a high contrast MRI of the head, and a high contrast CT scan of the torso (pelvis and chest). I got a high definition MRI just a few hours later.

That appointment launched us on a non-stop medical treadmill that lasted two weeks. We felt like we'd been shot out of a shot gun. The good thing was that Dr. R prescribed steroids for me, which reduced the swelling so I could communicate again.

When the neurologist called later that week, he had some concerns about my scan. He told us that I had an appointment the following Monday with Dr. S – an oncologist. No one had mentioned "cancer" yet, but seeing an oncologist couldn't be good.

The following week, the oncologist told me I had a mass on my lower left lung and some fluid in the chest cavity, along with a small cyst on my liver. They also noticed that my lymph nodes were just above normal in size. Dr. S set up appointments for me to get a PET scan and a biopsy, and meet with a radiation specialist and a neurosurgeon. He also ordered a complete blood work-up, which we somehow accomplished all during the shortened Thanksgiving week.

Believe me, Thanksgiving Day was a welcome reprieve from the "medical world." My kids had been staying with their dad through this craziness, and I still didn't have anything concrete to tell them except that I had a brain tumor, along with some other ones.

They didn't know what was going on, but I didn't want to scare them prematurely, because I didn't know either. Dan cooked up a fabulous Thanksgiving Day dinner for us. But my Friday appointment was hanging over us all.

Finally, the moment came when I received the diagnosis: Stage IV lung cancer that had spread to my brain. The oncologist felt we needed to get the tumor removed as soon as possible.

Dan drove us to an indoor conservatory filled with fresh flowers and walking paths. At my request, he made phone calls to some friends and family members. I felt so overwhelmed, I was numb. I didn't know what to think or what to say. Everything in my mind and heart felt stuck.

When we finally got home, we got a call letting us know that the neurosurgeon had an operating time open up on Monday – in three days. This catapulted us back into the whirlwind of trying to get a pre-operative physical and get scheduled for surgery. I even made an appointment with my attorney friend for Saturday at a coffee shop to update my will.

On the Monday after Thanksgiving, Dan and I reported early to the hospital to have my brain tumor removed. The hospital staff assured me that my surgeon was a superstar, and that I was in good hands.

For three weeks, I hadn't stopped. I may have prayed, but felt confident that many were praying for me.

Surgery went well. I was out of intensive care in record time. But the biopsy showed that the brain tumor was cancerous, and that the primary cancer site was in my lungs.

Once I got home from the hospital, life slowed down a bit. At least for awhile. My friend, Andrea, had started a blog site to keep friends and family members updated during my crisis. It was overwhelming reading the comments and encouraging words.

I also started writing the updates myself. Suddenly, I had a forum to process my journey in the best way I knew how – writing. I'd been keeping diaries and journals since I was seven years old. Writing was the way I reflected on and processed my life. It was perfectly natural for me to detail this new journey in the same way. What was different was that I got immediate responses.

The words from friends and family offered me incredible support and encouragement. The kindness and prayers offered on my behalf strengthened me to be able to keep going.

From here on, I'll share the thoughts I had along the way throughout the first year following my diagnosis.

My prayer is that somehow as you read, you'll feel a new hope in your own life.

Winter

November 27

Suzy has come through surgery with "flying colors!"

Doctors say they removed the entire tumor and that Suzy is making remarkable strides toward recovery. One doctor said, "Suzy's healthy, strong and young," and that he believes her body will recover quickly from this procedure.

Suzy has been moved from intensive care to a regular room. No worries with her "new digs." She has a remarkable view of the cities and a wonderful nursing staff.

Please call to encourage Suzy and lift her spirits!

November 30

Note from Suzy: I'm overwhelmed by all the love, prayers and support. I'm home today and I feel pretty good.

We've got a week right now for me to recoup before the sutures are removed — a time to collect treatment info for the next phase. So this week we've got some big decisions. Wisdom. Direction. Focus. That's what we need. And then to charge ahead into the critical next steps.

Thanks for all the care. I am truly blessed.

December 3

Thanks to everyone for the outpouring of support.

It's been 10 days since the lung biopsy results came back. I look at my scans, and can't believe my body has betrayed me like this, or rather that this invasive thing has lodged inside me.

There's no cure for lung cancer. I can't get over that. They can shrink tumors and cancer markers, but there's never a guarantee that it's just gone. Left untreated, it can go quick. With other therapies, they say I can still be here in two years — some are. I guess the advantage is that lung cancer is so common that there are a lot more options to help both extend your life as well as to live and enjoy it. But doctors speak in averages and "best case and worst case" scenarios. They don't know how I'll respond. I want a miracle.

At the University of Minnesota there are several clinical studies I can get into where they're using edgy drugs — one works well for female non-smokers. That's hopeful. But how does life change when a two-year plan is suddenly no longer short-term, but the time you get to do your life?

This still hasn't sunk in yet. I still really don't feel sick.

December 5

A loving friend, Marilyn, gave me a copy of "Kitchen Table Wisdom" yesterday. An M.D. and also chronically ill, author Rachel Remen says that:

> *"Expertise is not clairvoyance. As experts, we only deal with probability and not specific outcome. Like most people who do this sort of work, I've seen that the prognosis may not be the reality any more than the map is the territory the blueprint, or the building."*

The prognosis may not be the reality.
I like that.

I have a consultation at a radiation clinic tomorrow that's much closer to home than the one that's downtown. I'll get the sutures in my head out in a few days and the go ahead for further treatment. I'm scheduled at the Mayo Clinic in Rochester, Minn., next week. I check in at 6:45 a.m.

They'll do blood work, have all my scans, etc., and again come up with options. That will be another roadmap. Hopefully, there will be some overlap in the plans.

I'll likely start the radiation on my head late next week. I told the girls last night that I'd lose my hair. Elisa, my 11-year-old, suggested, "Maybe you should just stay in the house." But, rethinking, she thought a cool scarf would work. I thought maybe a scarf with one of my favorite baseball caps over it — like a red silky one with my new black Lion King hat. Christmassy. She wasn't sure about that one.

December 6

Today felt like a regular day. As usual, I woke up at 4:30 a.m., and then walked on the treadmill for 20 minutes (which I haven't done for a couple of weeks). Got dressed for work, the kids off to school and hopped in the car.

OK, so Dan drove me to an all-morning radiation oncologist appointment, which isn't exactly normal. But from there I went to work, had lunch with my colleagues, and worked the rest of the afternoon.

It felt normal. Regular. I came home to a mailbox full of cards that had been forwarded to my home address from the hospital. What a greeting!

It should feel this way for a couple of weeks. A chance to catch my breath after a surreal 23 days. Looks like I'll start brain radiation for three weeks beginning Dec. 20. And then whatever chemo the docs mix up.

December 8

At my last Thursday radiation appointment, Dr. C said I'm the fifth non-smoking woman in her 40s that she's treated for lung cancer this year. They have no idea what's going on. Because it can take years to develop, the average person who gets diagnosed with lung cancer is aged 69. It's the second-most diagnosed cancer in both men and women (behind prostrate and breast). They don't know why non-smoking, younger women are getting this disease — but they offer environmental factors and stress as educated guesses.

I feel very fortunate to have the Mayo Clinic appointments next week. Many have shared with me how blessed we've been to get in there so quickly, and the outstanding care plan that we'll receive. I've heard lots of success stories.

A doctor at work suggested we take a long weekend now, before treatments begin and while I'm feeling good. Dan offered to whisk me off on a cruise or to a beach, but when there's only three to four days, I didn't want to spend two of them traveling.

We decided to go up to a lodge next weekend in Brainerd. Yes — it's winter in Minnesota. But it seems like it will be restful, there's a spa there with some comforting amenities, and it's away from medical appointments. Dr. C was very supportive. "Do your information gathering and then just go away for a few days," she said. "We can start when you get back."

So that's the plan for now, unless we get other instructions from Mayo.

December 9

Had a "normal" weekend. My son, Matt, had a Lego tournament in St. Louis Park on Saturday where his team took fifth out of 16 teams. Dan and I got a couple of tickets to see the Minnesota Timberwolves basketball team win on Saturday night, and we got the Christmas tree up today.

It's a tradition for the kids and me to put up the tree, sip egg nog and watch "Rudolph the Red-Nosed Reindeer." And we did it all. Plus, I have a holiday jigsaw puzzle that we usually put together. Matt and Elisa were determined and got the whole thing done today.

I'm going to work tomorrow, getting my sutures removed late afternoon, and then heading down to the Mayo Clinic for the early Tuesday appointments. The past few days have been a great respite from doctor appointments.

I continue to be overwhelmed and grateful for the collective acts of love from friends, family and neighbors. My sister drove up from Iowa and cleaned out my front closet; mom decorated for Christmas; dad fixed the door. The freezer that "showed up," along with groceries. The books, resources and stories of hope. Neighbors bringing dinner and helping with rides for the kids, a third-grade neighbor who wove me a hat, the outpouring of messages on this site, the offers to help in a million little ways. I feel carried.

Thank you doesn't scratch the surface of what it's meant.

December 12

I know you were all thinking about us at Mayo yesterday. I'm not sure what I expected there — I'd heard so many great things. Actually, I do know what I expected. I so wanted a doctor to look at me and say, "We've got a magic cure here that no one else has, and it's going to help you beat this thing."

I didn't get that.

But the trip was still valuable. Dan and I spent some time in their cancer education library where an incredibly helpful and caring staff made copies of all the articles and current research we wanted. They gave us reference materials and I visited an interactive site where I could listen to hopeful patient testimonials.

The other valuable thing was that now all my records and scans are in their system. Should I come to a crossroads decision at any time during my care, I can return to get some additional opinions.

I'd also hoped that some of their clinical trials would fit my situation, but none currently do. My recent surgery disqualifies me in most cases, plus I would have to receive all the treatments there — and Rochester is two hours from my house. Because I don't qualify, the decision is made.

We did show the doctor one trial that I can do at the University of Minnesota, and he thought it would be a good fit for me. We're going to finish all the paperwork on that one, knowing I can drop out at any time. I need to let the decision on this one simmer for awhile. And I have time. Chemo won't start until late January. Although the drug — Avastin — is tested and approved, I don't know if I want to be a lab rat.

The gray-haired doctor was empathetic and teary. Although he didn't say it, what came clearly across to me is this: "It's not fair that you got this. You shouldn't have gotten this. And there's not enough in my medical arsenal to look at you and confidently say that you can beat it."

Again, these weren't his words — just the message I received in a million other ways.

It was a kind of downer day.

But today's a new day. On my drive in to work, I talked to Diane, a college roommate. She told me about a woman now in her 50s who had the same situation as I do. Her lung cancer diagnosis was five to eight years ago.

Diane confessed that Anita looks a bit more weathered than her age would suggest after everything her body went through, but that she is grounded, amazing, and has the depth of someone who's walked up to death's door and then turned around, refusing to go in. A success story.

Spent the day at work writing, returning phone calls and emails, and planning an oral history interview with an 87-year-old retired scientist for the day after tomorrow.

There were huge chunks of time when the weight of this was lifted from my spirit.

That's a good thing. A great thing. A gift.

December 14

The past two mornings while I've been walking on the treadmill, I read 50 pages into a book that my sister sent me: "Beating Cancer with Nutrition." Everything in this book makes so much sense, and the survival stories are amazing. Thank you, Lori!

I'd asked one doctor what I should be eating to prep my body for the upcoming treatments. She said, "Oh, just a balanced diet. The food pyramid." I was suspicious.

Amidst the wealth of information in this book, one line leaped out at me. "Sugar feeds cancer." Yikes. I know that the way they discovered where my actively growing cancer cells were was through a PET scan. They injected me with radioactive sugar juice, and then did an MRI an hour later. The active cancer cells glowed because they were gobbling up the sugar at a rapid rate. I read that cancer cells metabolize sugar at three to five times the rate of healthy tissue.

I've exercised my whole life. The meals I eat are healthy. But I do love those high-end desserts. Great chocolate, fresh-baked cookies and brownies, Cold Stone ice cream. It's all tasty comfort food. But I don't want to feed the cancer. I can't afford to.

I talked to a woman yesterday who is very knowledgeable about nutrition and disease. She advised me to go as sugar-free as possible.

What I've read in some books is that when you cut back on all that refined sugar, you stabilize your blood sugar and starve the cancer cells. Then, when chemo starts, they chow down on the chemicals, making treatment more effective. In the meantime, lower sugar helps the healthy cells be healthier — often reducing the icky side effects that come along with chemo.

I can't ignore that. So even though I love my chocolate, I decided it's not worth it. There's so much of this that I can't control. But I can control what I eat. Dan and I will keep reading about what I should be eating to rev up my immune system, and I'll take baby steps.

But yesterday I went the whole day without all those nummy Christmas treats. I need to redefine them not as "treats" but as — to me — poison.

Because I already exercise and make lots of good choices, I don't have to turn my life upside down. But this will be a change.

Pray that I can decide to say no. I have nothing to lose, and only quality of life to gain.

December 15

Overwhelmed

I'm sitting this morning amidst about a dozen flowers and plants that I've received from family and friends. The cut flowers are just starting to look a bit worse for the wear — but it has been nearly three weeks since my surgery!

I'm also sitting here with a basket filled with cards, along with gift cards and gas cards, books, and a few CDs. I have a generous gift certificate from "Let's Dish" from my friends at work. You've emailed links and Web resources that have been really helpful.

I know amazingly quality people. In that respect, it's not the outpouring of support that has surprised me, but just the sheer quantity. Thank you to all of you — I'm not sure I'll get written thank-you notes out, but I've been thanking people when we talk by phone, email, or see each other in person.

What has been most overwhelming, however, is the generosity of folks I don't think I've ever met. My understanding is that someone I don't know is the one who purchased the new garage freezer. I have a Subway gift card from a work colleague whom I met briefly after she heard me speak once. A local pizza takeout place donated a $35 gift certificate. I've gotten cards from a couple of people who I can't quite place.

And last night, Jenni, a neighbor who works with some of my other neighbors at Matthew's elementary school, brought over dinner. We said hello as new friends for the first time at my front door.

That's amazing. My heart is both humbled and ever so grateful.

We're coming up on Christmas here — and it's so easy to be cynical about the consumerism, and always-bad news that we see in headlines and hear on the news daily.

But all of you have tangibly demonstrated a very different story. None of you can control this disease in me any more than I can. But you want to help, and are reaching out in so many practical ways.

I so want to beat this so I can be on the giving end someday, too.

Medical update

I saw my original oncologist on Friday. He confirmed that a clinical trial currently being offered at the University of Minnesota (the only one I even qualify for) would be perfect for me. He said, "Do it." He said he would treat me the exact same way, only he'd have to use the trial drug later, rather than earlier — like the trial would do. The trial drug is an approved treatment.

Plus in the trial, that drug would be free for me — the drug company pays for it. And this is one of the more spendy ones — $3,000 per round. I think I'd get six rounds. Some health insurances pay more than others, leaving me with co-pays either way. He was very affirming that it would be a good, safe decision — one with which he's seen good results.

We've been in contact with the University, and are moving forward with it for now. Chemo would likely start toward the end of January.

You may not hear from me for a few days. Dan is whisking me away to a lodge up near Brainerd around noon today. Between now and lunchtime, however, Matt's got two basketball games, Katlynn's got dance rehearsal for Christmas Eve service, and Elisa's returning from a sleepover birthday party. But once we get out of town, we'll get to stay until Tuesday.

I'm not sure how available Internet access will be. But I'm looking forward to a few foo-foo services like a massage and pedicure, and connecting with long-time friends Mark and Elizabeth, who started a church in that area.

Today I am a red head!

Actually it's been a few days. I ran in to see my long-time stylist (more than 10 years) on Friday night to get my hair shortened up. I'm always in for my "cut and color" this time of year to cover up the straggly grays. Kind of missed that this year given the recent events.

She looked at the inch or so of growth since my last "touch up" and said, "Can you come back tomorrow? I can put some color on." I was a bit hesitant to add color to hair that likely will disappear in three weeks. But she said it was her treat.

So, after Matt's basketball game on Saturday, Dan and I headed over. Since this was a temporary endeavor, everyone was encouraging me to go bold! Dan actually picked out the color — 507 - R. It looked a bit orangey on the sample, but since she was adding it to my dark hair, I was assured I wouldn't look like a carrot. I'm pretty conservative when it comes to my hair — ask my boss, Tess.

But it turned out great! It's really short in back — longer on top to cover up my incision. She wrote down the color just in case I ever wanted to do this for real in the future. Thanks again, Sue.

December 18

This has been a great three days. We drove up to Grandview Lodge, near Brainerd, on Saturday, and are going home this morning.

Obviously, it's the off-season, so we had the place to ourselves. Both Dan and I enjoyed a few of the spa services — namely hot stone massages. I also convinced Dan to get his first manicure. I doubt he'll ever admit to getting one, but I must say that his hands look very well-groomed.

Ahhhh!

These have been perfect days — just what the doctor ordered. I've lounged around reading a lot. Headed over to the fitness center for leisurely workouts. Steamed at the spa. Got ready in the morning while sitting (who does that?) at a vanity that had drapes with fringe. Yesterday, I think it was 11:30 a.m. by the time I was ready for the day.

Can you imagine taking five hours from the time you get up until you're ready for work? What a luxury.

I finished my "Kitchen Table Wisdom" book by Rachel Remen — and highly recommend it for anyone else you know who is facing illness. Powerful, inspiring stories. And I'm halfway through my nutrition book — which continues to motivate me. Today I start Day 6 on my treat ban. It hasn't been so bad.

What's funny is that I'm actually eating more real food. Before this, I probably ate 500 calories or so of treats throughout the day. A cookie here. A couple of chocolate truffles or chocolate kisses there. OK, maybe more than just a couple. On the drive up, we bought foot-long subs at Subway. I ate my usual six-incher — but then I didn't have a cookie or other nummy dessert. I was still hungry, so I ate the other six inches! I was amazed.

Last night, we visited long-time friends Mark and Elizabeth. They moved to Brainerd four years ago to start a church called "The Journey North." Elizabeth outdid herself, as usual, by serving up a great dinner — and we had fun catching up with them and their four kids — two of whom I'd never met.

It's been a great weekend. I must say, I'm glad there isn't a lot to do right now up here besides gaze at the frozen, snow-covered ice sheet called Gull Lake. If there were too many attractions, Dan and I might try to do the "Florida vacation revisited." That would mean seeing and doing everything, dawn to dusk, collapsing in a heap, and then doing it all again the next day.

This weekend wasn't like that. I'm grateful.

December 19

In case you're ever on "Who Wants to be a Millionaire," or some other game show — here's some trivia. What's the cost for brain surgery these days? I got my first "Explanation of Benefits" from my health insurance company. You know the one. It says, "This is NOT a bill."

The straight out hospital bill to the insurance company for my three-and-a-half day hospital jaunt was more than $53,000. To be precise — $53,709.82.

Woah! Lots more than my C-section with Katlynn in 1994. Of course, the insurance company wheels and deals and negotiates that cost down, and I'm only responsible for my in-patient per day co-pay. But geez — that's one big chunk of change!

December 21

A poem I wrote nearly four years ago has been bumping around in my head. After scrounging around a bit, I finally found it. I wrote it from the depths when facing the end of my 17-year marriage. Reading it today, it takes on new, but still very valuable meaning as I take the first steps on this next "long road."

Today, I'm not quite in the despair that I was then, but I'm sure I'll have my days.

Unwelcome Road

I'm plodding down the pathway
Of a long, unwelcome road.
Throughout this stormy journey,
I've acquired a heavy load.

I'm someone I don't recognize
I'm not myself at all,
I see the world through weariness,
A hazy, numbing pall.

My destination's hidden
I can't return to what's behind,
But somewhere in the middle
Is a life that now is mine.

I never chose this journey,
I don't embrace it now,
Healing's off on the horizon,
Closure's out of reach somehow.

At least my feet are moving,
But grief will still arrive
Though pain is inconvenient
Tears tell me I'm alive.

Then I hear a quiet murmur
As I move through shadowed blur.
Could it be a breath of hopefulness?
An optimistic stir?

*"I'm your destination
I'm the road beneath your feet.
I'm the water that sustains you
I'm every light you meet.*

*"I know your face, beloved,
You are intimately known.
I'm your compass. I'm your partner.
You do not walk alone."*
(2004)

Thanks to each of you for allowing God to bless me through you by being "every light I meet." Every conversation, card, gift, prayer, and kindness is another light in my day.

December 22

I'm looking out my kitchen window at a perfectly frosted scene — a good inch of coarse, puffy snow sitting atop my deck chairs, railings and trees. It's so perfect.

And I'm surrounded by three angels — the little Willow Tree wooden sculptures that kind hearts have gifted me along the way: Hope, Courage and Miracles. I love them.

Two of my 15 radiation treatments are behind me, and now I get a four-day break. The first day was really long, only because the doctors and technicians were doing X-rays, pointing, marking, fidgeting and shifting a millimeter here and a millimeter there to get everything adjusted just right. I'm glad they're being so precise — aiming at the brain and avoiding all the other important stuff in my head like eyes, ears, sinuses, mouth, etc.

It was a bit nerve-wracking, though, because it took so long. I'm lying down with a plastic mesh "Hannibal Lechter" mask on my face that is clamped to the table. The technicians are great, very soothing and telling me exactly what they're doing, what the lights and sounds are, and asking me if I'm doing OK, to which I can only reply with "Uh-huh," or "uh-uh."

The rest of my body is totally free, but I can't open my eyes or move my head. I kept thinking, "What if I have to cough?" "Or sneeze?" "What if I have an itch?" Bizarre. I just tried to relax and breathe. Breath prayers. On the inhale I prayed, "The healing breath of God." And on the exhale, "Blowing the cancer away." I don't know how long I was in there, but it seems I prayed a long time — a good 20 plus minutes. This really wouldn't be so bad on any other body part except the brain.

The actual treatment was only 15 to 20 seconds on each side of my head. They assured me that after the first session, I'd be in and out really fast. They were right. Yesterday it was 10 minutes from the time I checked in to walking out the door.

I asked when my hair might begin to drift away — they said around session 10, which is January 7 or so. So I'll have hair through the holidays.

Last night I dreamed I lost a tuft of hair.

December 23

As my kids are reminding me, it's Christmas Eve Eve. I talked to my sister in northeast Iowa this morning and she's snowed in. They had a ton of snow yesterday, and now wind. Five-foot drifts. Not good. I'm disappointed that she can't come up, but next weekend should work.

Dan got some new photos posted on my Web site this morning — my hair's not THAT red. And for all of you who are far away — that's Dan!

December 24

Today's my favorite day. I love the anticipation before Christmas Day — the wrapped gifts, the music, the magic. I make wild rice soup (even though the kids hate it) and my grandma's Christmas cupcakes, which we smother in butter sauce. Christmas Eve service. Drinking egg nog by the lit tree. Reading "Twas the Night Before Christmas" and the Bible story from Luke 2. Opening one present.

We just finished our third Christmas puzzle of the season — another family tradition. Early tomorrow I'll sit by the tree with Good Earth tea one last time before the bustle begins. By 7 a.m. on Christmas Day it's chaos. And a mess! Today is the best day.

Blessings to all of you on this joyful day when we pause to celebrate with family and friends the miracle of Immanuel — "God with us."

Merry Christmas.

December 26

Doctor's reports are descriptively distant. I typically get visit notes a few weeks down the road following an appointment. When my sutures were removed, the letter included, "Suzanne is a delightful woman in no distress. Her gait is steady. Her speech is fluent. She asks excellent questions."

Sounds like I got an A.

Today, however, I received the summary notes from our Mayo visit. Some lines jumped out. "She is a life-time never smoker." "She has recovered nicely from her craniotomy." "She's a well-nourished, well-hydrated female. She is alert and oriented times three.

What on earth does that mean?

Other comments, however, are of great concern. I knew there was cancer in my left lung, but I guess I'd not officially heard nor read about the extent.

"A large mass in the left lower lobe, measuring approximately 10 cm, with a few other satellite nodules around the mass. A small, left-sided pleural effusion was also seen (it's in the lung fluid). Very small (5 mm) indeterminate nodule was seen in the right upper lobe."

"Unfortunately, given her advanced stage of disease, her prognosis remains guarded at this point."

I have to remember: The prognosis isn't necessarily the reality.

Today was radiation treatment 3 — the last one will be on January 14. After that, it will be 1 to 2 weeks until I can start chemo for the lung. My diagnosis came nearly a month ago. That means it will be two months from when I first learned about this until we can attack the source.

New, urgent prayer request: Pray that in this next month the cancerous cells in my lung will go into complete hibernation. They need to just go to sleep. They can't grow, spread, or do anything else to me. In fact, shrinking would be good. Disappearing even better.

The prognosis isn't necessarily the reality. Help me remember that.

December 28

I had coffee last week with Suzanne, a designer who freelances for our group and other departments at work. I've known her throughout my four-plus year stint back at full-time work.

She was in Sri Lanka in December when she heard about my news. Being both creative, thoughtful and a nine-year breast cancer survivor, she brought back the coolest gift for me.

I opened the handmade card, which had a peacock on it, as well as a gorgeous hand-batiked scarf-like wall hanging, also depicting a peacock. She'd printed out some info on the animal symbolism in different cultures and religions.

In Christianity, the peacock represents immortality.

In Buddhism, the culture of Sri Lanka, "peacocks are said to have the ability of eating poisonous plants without being affected by them ... By eating poison, the peacock's body becomes healthy and beautiful ... and the colors of his feathers become bright and his body healthy."

As someone who also has had her bout with chemotherapy, she said the peacock symbolizes the process. Although medical science uses toxins to attack the cancer cells, the result can be health and beauty.

What a great symbol for me to hang on to next month as I start down that road. It's a visual representation of one of the many paths God can use for healing. Thanks, Suzanne.

December 28

Wig School 101

Am I a wig person? I haven't decided yet. But acting on the recommendations of a few friends and health care professionals, I made an appointment to meet with a "wig specialist" today.

Twila has apparently been a beautician for many, many years. All glammed up, she had two-inch pink acrylics and, of all things, a youthful, spiky blonde wig. She told me that she's been wearing wigs for 40 years.

I sat in her chair and told her I needed Wig School 101. She said, of course, that human hair was the best — it can be curled, permed and highlighted, and you can't beat the durability. A well-cared for wig could last several years. "They start at $1,000," she said. I said I was open. But really I wasn't open at all — like I would ever spend that much on hair. Get real.

She brought out a longish, brunette one and flopped it on my head like a mop. Of course, she would fit it and cut it so that it would be perfect for me. I just didn't see it.

So she brought in another one — synthetic, and only $599. It was darker than I'd want, but she assured me that it could be ordered in any color and that this color was definitely not me. I wasn't crazy about the cut either. The sides and back were OK, but it felt a bit beehive-like on top. I don't think so.

The next one was $449. Much closer to the color my hair is normally — when it's highlighted and foiled, that is. Cute, sassy. It made these little flippy things in back that my curly hair never manages to do.

Twila left for a bit, and I kept looking in the mirror. It kind of felt like me. It might be nice to have hair to go to work or to a restaurant. I mean, can I really wear hats, scarves and turbans for six to 12 months?

Behind me, the elderly lady, who had been silent up until this point, whispered, "That's looks really cute, honey."

My "wig specialist" returned, and I told her it felt right. She proceeded to poke and fuss with it, showing me all the hip ways I could arrange it.

"Two things," she said. "Don't lean too close to a hot stove. The synthetic fibers can melt. And this part in the back? Once it's been rubbing on the collars of your coats or scarves — it can get fuzzy. But don't you worry about that — just bring it in and I can resteam it, or we can just trim it up."

"Do you want to wear it home?"

Uh, no. Taking it home would mean that my hair really would fall out. And I'm still days away from that. Plus that's a lot of money for hair. The Cancer Society has some for $40, but I've heard from reliable resources that they're itchy — and that you get what you pay for.

But she did promise to hold it for me. That way I could call her next week, zip in to have it fit, trimmed and styled, and I'd be good to go.

I told this tale to Diane, my college friend who now lives in Colorado. She thought it was absurd to have to pay for hair, and suggested I ask the technicians who administer the radiation and chemo to ante up to help with the cost.

That seems only fair.

January 4

T-minus five days and counting — until hair drift

It's been a few days since the last update — but I've had all kinds of thoughts milling around. More on that later.

But for now, my head itches! Today will be radiation treatment 8 of the 15 sessions. The therapists said my head would feel a bit irritated, like a sunburn. That's exactly how it feels. Like when you fry your shoulders on that first day outside in the summer, and then try to wear a shirt over it. Ouch.

Very tender, especially to the touch.

The radiation therapists also told me this is the first sign of pending hair loss.

I asked them if they feel bad for inflicting this treatment that causes such a dramatic side effect. They said, "Yes! But we try to focus on the benefit of the treatment. And remember, it's just temporary."

Easy for them to say.

January 5

I have to put in a shameless plug for the new movie, "The Kite Runner." The novel is probably in my top five best books of all time. I gave away half a dozen of this book as gifts — and men and women equally loved it. It's by Khaled Hosseini.

Dan read it too, and loved it. But we were a bit skeptical, knowing how Hollywood can mess up novels.

We saw it last week — if you read this book, you have to see this movie. It adds all the sights and sounds of Afghanistan and stays true to the powerful story. Admittedly, most of the theater was filled with the aged 40-plus crowd, but there was not a dry eye in the theater after the poignant ending.

If any of you haven't read the book, and see the movie anyway — I'm curious as to what you think. It seems the movie can stand solidly on its own, but I'm not the best judge.

Let me know.

January 6

This body journey has some quirky parallels to pregnancy. I remember during pregnancy feeling like I was on a rollercoaster ride with my body, never fully knowing what might be around the next bend.

Oh, swollen ankles. That's new. And a spot of heartburn. Never had that before. Strange new sensations that made me realize that I was truly on a rollercoaster ride and just had to go with it until the attendant let me get off at the end.

Hair today, gone tomorrow

That's sort of what this has been like. Yesterday, there was more than the usual amount of hair in the sink, and on the comb. I wouldn't say it's coming out in "tufts" or "clumps" yet, but when I run my fingers through it, I certainly find "multiple strands."

On the bright side, I calculated what I spend on haircuts, foil highlights, shampoo, conditioner, gel, hair spray and just "fuss" time in a year — and it totals several hundred dollars and many hours.

I wish this little phase would be done already so I can stop thinking about it and just move on.

January 7

Quick question. I've been encouraged by all the books I've been given — which, by the way, I'm plowing through very quickly.

Who sent me "Peace, Love & Healing, " by Bernie Siegel, M.D.? I LOVE this guy, and will likely be sharing quotes frequently. He's a doctor who totally gets the mind/body connection.

He suggests being open and aware to what God and life are teaching us, and to get to the real questions: "How can I live and understand the moment?"

"Disease can be our spiritual flat tires," he says, "disruptions in our lives that seem to be disasters at the time but end in redirecting our lives in a meaningful way."

These "flat tires" don't have to be as drastic as cancer, but can include grief, loss, disappointments, challenges, redirects, or even minor illnesses. This is a great reminder for all of us to pay attention to those life lessons that cross our paths every day, to learn from them, and make important course corrections.

January 8

I'm shedding like a cat. It started last Saturday, and I've watched every day in a sort of morbid fascination as it drifts off my head, fills the comb, and covers my collar.

Yesterday, I "pasted" my hair on with hair spray and went hatless to work. In a panic, I emailed Chris from the knitting club (an employee club at work) to bring over a few hats that were finished. Knowing I was having radiation, Chris had asked the group to help out. Good thing. My hair was going fast! So she brought two.

This morning more and more hair came out. I asked Elisa, "Hat or no hat?" She eyed my much-thinned, hair-sprayed scalp and said, "Hat." So I wore a purple one with my bangs and curly sideburns still intact.

When I got in to work, my desk was covered with more "hand-knit with love" hats. Thank you!

At radiation later, I took my hat off and the inside of it was covered with hair. So I called Sue, who cuts my hair. Help!

I just got back from her studio, and she trimmed everything down to one inch, except for the little fringe that can still peak under a hat. I wasn't ready to just shave it.

This is so weird.

January 10

As I'm digesting everything I've been reading, I'm hearing again and again about the value in liking your doctors. Not just trusting their expertise, but liking who they are.

I've spent a few hours over the past six weeks with my radiation oncologist in Maple Grove. She's just a bit younger than I am, and Harvard trained. Intensely curious as to why people go into oncology to begin with, she ended up answering the question before I asked.

When I met with her this week, I asked whether or not she was a reader. "Yes!" Have you read "The Kite Runner?" "Yes, I loved it!" Have you seen the movie? "Yes, I loved it!" Then we talked about what was great about both.

We agreed that the sights and sounds of the movie were tremendous — the music, the kite scenes. Then she said, "It was so great to see the freedom the Afghans felt while flying kites, even though they are so oppressed. That's why I like working with patients — when people begin to have physical limitations, it's amazing to watch their spirits soar!"

I like her. A lot.

January 11

Cancer Club

So this will be Day 4 of wearing a hat to work. And I must admit, it's a little awkward. It is winter in Minnesota, after all — so I don't mind wearing a hat while I'm walking around wearing my winter coat.

But once the coat is off, it's a little different. It's not like there's even a handful of women roaming the halls wearing hats indoors because it's trendy. It feels like a hat is a badge that broadcasts my membership in the Cancer Club.

Of course, I'm grateful for the encouragement from my co-workers and all the hats knit with love so I can have some fashionable options.

But I don't have visible signs of "cancer." Rather it's the treatment that keeps changing my outward appearance — and this week, it's been daily. My hair gets shorter and thinner, and my forehead looks red like a tomato from the radiation — plus it's sore.

Sigh.

I've been hearing from a few of my classmates from our 1985 Bethel England Term. Thank you. I'm sorry to have missed our fall reunion, but want to make the next one. Has it really been more than 20 years since we were traipsing through the fens with our Wellies and visiting literary shrines?

(That means walking through the wetlands wearing our rain boots, and visiting the birthplaces, homes and gravestones of many English, Scottish and Welsh authors.)

January 14

Matt's birthday

Call me crazy, but Dan and I pulled off a sleepover party last Saturday night for Matthew's 10th birthday. It was Shaun's weekend to have the kids. Shaun is the father of my children and my ex-husband.

Matt's birthday is January 15. Next weekend is booked up, and Matt really wanted a sleepover party. At least the girls would already be at their dad's house — Matt's sleepovers never work when the girls are in the house.

I'm not a night person. At my best, I still crash by 10 and wake up early, and this week I've been particularly sleepy. But Dan came to the rescue and helped me pull it off.

We took six fourth grade boys to Grand Slam for lazer tag, bumper cars, batting cages, pizza and video games for three hours, then came home for snacks, cake and presents.

I was asleep by 11 p.m. Dan stayed up until 3 a.m. with the boys. After that, I was glad to get up to make bacon and pancakes for breakfast.

Even so, I took a four-hour nap that afternoon. I hate needing so much sleep. And I'm not particularly fond of getting a good night's sleep, but still not waking up with a spark. Fatigue is an annoyance, but I know my body's trying to heal from the radiation and fight off the cancer.

I'm trying to pay attention to my body's signals. But it's hard.

January 15

Today's the last day of radiation. When I met with the radiation doctor yesterday, however, she reminded me that side effects will continue to escalate this week and then start to fade a bit next week. Like the sunburn, itchy head and fatigue.

We're already lining up the chemo appointments with a new-to-me Pakistani oncologist, and the before-treatment scans.

While I get two weeks off to recover before chemo actually starts, all the prep work will be going on so I can take that next step.

We're targeting January 31 as the start date for chemo.

My friend, Mary (and her 3-year-old, Sam), stopped to have lunch with me at work yesterday — armed with scarves. After we ate, I tried them on in the bathroom to see what worked and what didn't. Then she left to go tackle the stores again. Later, she brought me a collection of brimmed hats — which seemed to work best. Gives me that reporter look.

Thank you! Although accessorizing adds one more step in the whole morning "getting ready" process, it's needed at the moment.

Happy birthday, Matt! My "little" boy turns 10 today.

January 17

My lungs were achy yesterday morning on the way into work. I don't know why, because later they felt fine. But rather than worrying about something ominous, I pictured my body waging battle against the cancer cells, and the cancer cells not being pleased, putting up a bit of a fight themselves, but ultimately giving in. Kind of like the little sword battles on Matthew's computer games.

Also, I was pleasantly surprised to get to work and see Tess, my boss, colleague and friend, wearing a hat. She was meeting with someone, but I gave her a silent "thumbs up." Soon, more of my co-workers were donning hats — apparently, it was hat day!

Since we're a corporate communication and public relations group, everyone looked very "media-ish" as we sat around the conference table in our area.

Thanks, guys. Very stylish.

January 18

I've seen several lists like this one, but this is the most concise. It's based on psychologist Warren Berland's study of long-term survivors, as described near the beginning of the book "Peace, Love and Healing," by Bernie Siegel.

Characteristics of survivors

The ability to express anger

The individual who gets angry, calls the doctor for help when told he or she is incurable, or displays righteous indignation when not treated with respect is more likely to survive than the individual who becomes depressed, goes home and lies down to die.

Willingness to learn and make lifestyle changes

The person who attends workshops, reads books and changes his or her life because of what he or she learns is also more likely to survive.

Survivors pay attention to what they feel is the "right" life for them. This is not about being selfish, but about saving your life by living the life you desire, and not the one imposed upon you.

Spirituality

A resource that brings with it peace and support in the most difficult times. It is very difficult, but very healing at times to leave your troubles to God. Siegel doesn't use the word religion in this context because he says the rules and practices of some religions can lead to guilt and problems of healing. God is not the problem. God and adversity are the teachers. Thus survival behavior eliminates the victim role.

God and adversity are the teachers. That's what's mulling around in my head. What is this teaching me? Why is this in my life now?

January 19

Can you say "sleep?"

Last night, I stretched out to read a few pages of a book at 7 p.m. I ended up waking up at midnight, rolling over and getting up at 7 a.m. this morning. And then I slept for two hours this afternoon. I am a slug.

In the meantime, Dan was getting the girls to a hockey game and managing the kids' friends who were in and out. All while I was comatose. What a fun Friday night date I am.

Matt, my son, had basketball games this morning and made two baskets in one game. This was quite an accomplishment for him, since all last season he'd only scored one basket. He doubled his scoring already for this year, and this was only the mid-season tourney. Yay for him!

January 22

A happy note

Dan and I are getting married on Thursday. That's right – the day after tomorrow on Jan. 24 (I like even numbers). The service will be short, sweet and small. At my house with a Cold Stone ice cream cake. Our pastor's daughter is dancing in a talent show that night, so he'll stroll in about 7:30 p.m.

It will be just the two of us, plus my kids – Katlynn (13), Elisa (11) and Matt (10) – Dan's 15-year-old son, Seth, and Steve, a high school friend of Dan's, along with Steve's wife, Jody. Weather permitting, my sister, Lori, will make the arduous trek from northeast Iowa, and I hope my friend, Mary.

My kids are with us that night, and they don't have school the next day. So Dan and I will get away late Friday to a bed and breakfast for a murder mystery. Once there, I will play Babs Blabs, a 1920s gossip columnist for a small town newspaper, and Dan will be a greedy Harvard law student.

I know many of you haven't met Dan, nor do you know much about him. I'll have to fill you in bit by bit, but here's a snippet.

In 2003, with divorce looming, I ran off to a silent retreat to cry buckets and write volumes. In a particularly potent moment, I scrawled off, "I will never get in a serious relationship with anyone who hasn't read Tolkien's 'Lord of the Rings' before he saw the movies!" This, perhaps, was the tangible metaphor for my desire for someone who shared some of my quirky (or as a colleague put it, "complex") interests.

Needless to say, very early on he revealed that not only had he read the book, but had done so multiple times. Ah, my heart!

January 26

Big week

We found a Wi-Fi Internet cafe in Buffalo this afternoon, so I could get online. I forgot my cell phone at home last night. Oops.

Our wedding was great. My house actually looked prettier than I thought it would, thanks to Dan buying and arranging pink and white flowers into bouquets.

My parents were involved in spirit — dad sent up a Randy Travis song for us to play, "Forever and Ever Amen," and mom wanted to send flowers. The day before the wedding, I had spontaneously stopped in at a florist's and selected flowers to wear on my head. When I picked it up, it was a little bigger than anticipated, but still pretty. So when I cascaded down the steps to greet guests, I introduced myself as "Athena, goddess of spring!" And the aroma followed me around all evening.

My sister, Lori, drove up and long-time friend, Mary. Dan's lifelong friends, Steve and Jody came too. Thanks for making the effort on a freezing cold day — I believe the thermometer here read 12 degrees below zero.

Our pastor, Eric, performed the ceremony, and Dan and I each said a few words. OK, more than a few. I read a poem I'd written that I adapted for the night, and I'll post that later. Dan read from I Cor. 13.

Mostly what I want to say today is thank you. Thank you for the outpouring of encouragement, prayers, love, support and positivity. It's beyond comprehension. And we're so grateful.

More big steps start next week, but today's not for that. Now we costume up for our big mystery dinner. I ended up being the murderer last time we did this — maybe this time it will be Dan.

Stay warm.

January 28

Back on the medical treadmill

I knew my morning would be spent at the clinic, but the day took an unexpected turn.

I got my brain MRI and high contrast CT scan (which meant I drank barium "berry smoothie" so that things would show up well). Then we met for the first time with Dr. M to talk about chemo. As far as side effects, he pretty much said I just need to do the first round to determine my baseline. Every drug is different. Every person is different.

For now, I'm still scheduled to start chemo at noon, three days from now.

In the meantime, they read my new scans. The brain one was "normal" for having a recent surgery. The chest one revealed that the tumor had grown slightly, about 5 mm one direction and 3 mm another, and that a few new small ones (3 mm) appeared on the right side of my lungs. That's happened in the past two months.

The concern of the moment, however, was the amount of fluid in my left lung. They immediately scheduled me to go to a downtown hospital to have it drained — a thoracentisis. So suddenly, we were there — and Dr. L drained 2 liters of fluid out through a tube in my back. Woah. I'd felt a bit sluggish over the weekend, a bit of heaviness in my chest, and tired of feeling tired.

I had no idea. I do feel better, but my chest is a bit twingy now that it's re-inflating some and filling in all those gaps.

I have a consultation late tomorrow with a thoracic surgeon to talk about fusing the inner and outer lung linings together using some mystery powder (sounds like glue to me) so that the lining won't refill. It sounds like it's fairly non-invasive, like today's procedure. Any new fluid would accumulate outside the lung and be washed away by the lymph system.

They're hoping to get this done this week as well — all before chemo would start. Whew. After what felt like a short reprieve, it seems I'm right back in the thick of things.

January 31

Change of plans

Dan and I are 10 minutes away from hopping in the car to go check into the hospital at 5:45 a.m.

Concerned about the fluid in my lung refilling, my docs had a pow-wow and wanted to make sure that the airways were clear and there was no place for the fluid to collect.

Once chemo starts, the immune system is weakened and the possibility of pneumonia increases. With fluid in my lung, it could be much more serious.

Rather than fusing the linings (which would require a few days in the hospital), we're doing day surgery. They'll put me out, and peek inside my lungs with cameras — I think they go through my back for this.

When the doctor is able to see what's going on, he can prop open one of the main bronchial tubes with a stent, drain the fluid that may have collected over the last three days, and add a little tube for external drainage. I'll be tapped like a tree.

My oncologist opted for this procedure because he doesn't want to delay chemo any longer from a hospital stay — we're rescheduled to start next week. The tumor secretes liquid, and my body is throwing liquid at the tumor — and hence the fluid. As the tumor shrinks, the issue should be lessened.

The procedure starts at 7:40 a.m. — not sure how long it will take. But then I have another appointment at noon, then they let me out to go home and recoup.

As much as this was a wrench in the week, it feels like the right thing to do — my lungs feel a bit achy now, so I think the fluid is reappearing.

Yesterday morning at this time it was 20 degrees below zero. Right now it's a balmy zero.

January 31

Still walking and talking

I can now add "thoracic surgery" to my medical resume.

The procedure this morning took around 90 minutes — a bit less than anticipated. The doctor took a firsthand look through a camera poked down my flexible air tube (used because I was already under general anesthesia). With all the fluid gone, the bronchial airway of concern was open, so he didn't need to put in a stent. The tumor was outside the airway, so he didn't laser anything.

They drained more fluid from my lung, and then inserted one end of a drainage tube into my lung cavity. The other end pokes out from the side of my body so we can drain any additional fluid that may accumulate. Actually, I've already determined that it will be Dan who does this, not me.

Chemo will start in four days — and the oncologist's concerns have been addressed. As chemo helps with tumor shrinkage, the fluid that it produces (and what my body throws at it to fight it) will reduce.

Today, I'm on some good narcotics (Percocet) and feel OK. When it starts to wear off, it feels like I got punched in the left side. Plus the air tube left me with a hoarse, raspy, sultry voice. Only for awhile.

> *"What lies behind us and what lies before us are tiny matters compared to what lies within us."*
>
> *—Ralph Waldo Emerson, American essayist & poet*

And, gratefully, what lies within me is faith, and who lies within me is God.

February 2

I pulled out this poem that I'd written just three years ago, on Dec. 31, 2004, and rewrote it a bit to read at our wedding last week. It might be familiar to some of you — I sent out the original version of "One Foot in the Joy" with my holiday letter that year.

That's the thing, isn't it? I had a really great year in many ways. Dan and I and our four kids took our dream Disney trip to Orlando; the girls danced at Epcot. So many great memories all year long. And then suddenly life changed. But the diagnosis doesn't change the fact that there were incredible times — I can't let one thing rob the joy from the many other precious moments and experiences.

The challenge for me — and for all of us — is to keep one foot grounded in the joy, while still trudging through the very real difficulties of life.

One Foot in the Joy

*Let's go on a treasure hunt
While we're together here.
Let's find the jewels we've stored away
And learn to keep them near.*

*No matter what our circumstance,
There's magic every day
When walking through a shadow,
Joy sustains along the way.*

*Its presence is a blessing,
If we always keep it near
And seek it in small places,
Then tuck it into tears.*

*Joy won't erase life's tragedy,
Or make hurt go away,
But nor does shadow cancel joy,
If you've invited it to stay.*

*So what joy lies deep within you?
What's twinkling in your soul?
God longs for us to seek it out.
Release its grace-filled flow.*

We've felt joy in a sunrise.
We've sensed it during prayer.
It sparkled in a child's eye,
Its imprint everywhere.

Now we spring into the future,
A new phase has arrived.
Let's pay attention to the moments,
That keep our hearts alive.

Today we travel forward,
Though life's trials seek to destroy,
But love and healing come from walking,
With one foot in the joy.

(2004)

February 4

"I think lung cancer found you, Mom."

That's what my daughter, Elisa (11), told me last night. "You're the healthiest person I know."

Regardless of the why, today we launch the counter-attack. What I know is that I check in around 9:15 a.m. and get labs drawn. They hook me up to an IV at around 10 a.m. and pre-medicate me with anti-nausea, anti-anxiety, anti-allergic reaction and probably anti-I-didn't-ever-want-to-have-to-do-this-in-my-life-but-here-I-am-anyway.

Besides Dan, I'm bringing today's crossword, a praise CD, a book, my peacock scarf and my laptop (just in case there's wi-fi).

If all goes OK, it should take just over two hours. After that, it's all unknown. My oncologist, Dr. M, just said to go through one round and see what it's like for me.

OK, here we go.

February 5

Round 1 behind me

Yesterday took longer than expected – we checked in at 9:30 a.m. and didn't get out of there until 4:30 p.m.

They used two different drugs: Taxol and Carboplatin. Both ran through an IV. First, they pre-medicated me for everything under the sun (after listening to pharmacists who alerted me to every side effect that could happen from now until eternity). The pre-meds took 30 minutes, the Taxol ran for three hours, and the Carboplatin ran for an hour.

So basically, they gave me a drug that can cause allergic reactions, and Benadryl and steroids so I don't have allergic reactions.

They gave me drugs that make me want to throw up, and then power drugs so I don't get nauseas. Steroids woke me up, Benadryl put me to sleep.

All in all, I felt OK. I sat in a recliner, watched the snow, logged in online and listened to music. After that I was bored and got up and walked around rolling my little IV stand with me. Dan was comfortable enough in his recliner and actually fell asleep for awhile. What a ride.

Surprisingly, I felt OK this morning. I walked on the treadmill for a mile, actually felt a little hungry, and had breakfast. The main thing they warned me about initially is nausea, but they pre-medicated me so much, it shouldn't hit me until tomorrow. That's what I'm banking on, although they also gave me more drugs to take in case it hits me early.

My face is flushed today, which the pharmacist told me would happen.

I met a woman at work who painted a hopeful picture of working through much of this process. She said her Day 2 was always good (from all the pre-meds), but she had lower energy on Day 3. She didn't feel nauseas, more like she had motion sickness.

She counseled me to take the anti-nausea drugs tomorrow as prescribed whether I thought I needed them or not. She usually stayed home that day and just preferred not moving.

So we'll see.

February 8

First Round Chemo Week: Day 5

What to say about this week. It's new to me to have to be so body aware. I have to ask myself, "How am I feeling?" Sometimes I don't know. So I walk a little on the treadmill while I read. How did that feel? OK? Time to take a shower, get ready. Eat breakfast. Now, how do I feel? Still pretty good. If I make it that far, I go in to work, which I did three days this week, including today. I used to just charge through the day and collapse in a heap at the end of it.

It's not unlike my emotional life. I cruise through tasks, ticking things off my achiever-mentality list. Someone asks, "How are you?" Although "fine" or "good" is what quickly pours out, I often wonder if I spoke in haste. Often I'm doing OK. Other times, maybe not. I need to pay more attention either way. I may not need to paint the big picture for all askers, but I should at least know – for my own sake.

Maybe this body thing also will help me better tune in to my emotional dial. Become more "heart aware." Notice more. It seems to me I should check in to the state of my emotions at least as frequently as I have to check in with my new aches and pains. It only makes sense.

Deep achy-ness has been my only real "symptom" this week. Starting on the evening of Day 3, I had a day or so of joint and muscle pain. When I described it to my co-workers as "floating twingies of sharp achy-ness," Grant commented that the phrase would make a great start for a country & western song.

All you musicians and poets out there can go ahead and use that one on me.

My kids will be at their dad's for the weekend starting tomorrow. I'm looking forward to a weekend with no expectations.

February 11

And now for something completely different....

Since 1998, I've made it my goal to read at least 12 books per year. In my most prolific year, I read 30. Last year, I read 23, and four already this year.

For anyone who's interested — here are some recommendations, in order read, not ranked.

Suzy's Annual Top Five

The Good Earth, by Pearl S. Buck

My Sister's Keeper, by Jodi Piccoult

Snow Flower and the Secret Fan, by Lisa See

A Thousand Splendid Suns, by Khaled Hosseini (author of The Kite Runner)

Eat, Pray, Love, by Elizabeth Gilbert (non-fiction)

Kitchen Table Wisdom, Rachel Naomi Remen, M.D. (non-fiction) – This one is hopeful and inspiring related to illness.

February 16

All is well

It's been a quiet week. I stayed out of clinics and doctors' offices and was at work every day. Except on the day I took Katlynn in to get antibiotics for a sinus infection she hasn't been able to kick.

February 20

I have a movie recommendation (my co-workers are tired of hearing me talk about this).

"August Rush"

Hadn't heard a thing about it, but saw it Saturday night at the cheap theater and LOVED IT. Brought Dan to it again Monday night, and he loved it too.

If music in any form has ever spoken to you in any way — you'll love this feel-great movie. I came home Saturday and ordered the eclectic soundtrack off Amazon for $9.99. Everything from gospel and classical, to street musicians and rock. Can't wait to get it.

We were celebrating my friend Mary's birthday when we saw the movie. I'd actually spent her 24th birthday with her exactly 20 years ago. We were on a staff trip out in Colorado with TreeHouse, the youth outreach of Family Hope Services, where we both worked.

We spent her birthday in Denver at the Casa Bonita restaurant. When I asked the colorful strolling musician to play a birthday song, he broke into "La Cucaracha." The cockroach? A birthday song? Who knew? We reminisced about that trip and marveled that it was so long ago. Unbelievable.

February 23

Cancer is a strange road

After doctors and tests day in and day out just three months ago, and daily brain radiation through mid-January, life has calmed down considerably.

What I find difficult, however, is how to plan my life. Should we get tickets to that? Well, it's toward the end of Round 4. Should be OK. What about the work event in early May? Well, it's just after Round 6. Chemo effects are supposedly cumulative. What if I don't feel good that day? What if I do?

I hate planning life based on how I might or might not feel. But I don't want to check out and say no to everything either.

Plan, live

I've been thinking about my college friend, Lori. She dealt with serious health issues from about age 15 until her death at age 37. I'm tired of this medical road after three months, and she dealt with it constantly for more than 20 years.

One thing I remember, though, is that she lived her life. She planned. She did. In college, she and I went to England with a group from Bethel College to study for a semester. She ended up returning three weeks sooner than the rest of us for health reasons, but she also explored and experienced Europe for three months and one week.

She and I got tickets to hear Italian tenor Andrea Bocelli sing — and we went. We had to walk slowly and rest often to get from the parking lot to our seats in the Excel Center in St. Paul, but she was there. And if she made plans and had to cancel them — so be it. Nine times out of 10, she was there.

It seems to me that fear of "what if" isn't a healthy way to live life — regardless of the number of days we have.

February 28

Round 2 chemo day

I'm sitting in my recliner at the cancer clinic, all hooked up in my window-laden, techno-savvy infusion room. Just got all my pre-meds through the IV, and now I'm receiving the three-hour Taxol infusion, followed by an hour of Carboplatin. It's a cocktail, mixing the drugs with saline.

My friend, Julie, in a labor of love, printed out all my journal entries from the Web and "scrapbooked" them. They're in a great album, with entries and extra decor on each page. One page has a close-up of a peacock's fanned tail. Wow, thank you.

Not just one thing

I don't think it was just one thing that created the environment within my body to allow cancer to cultivate. And I don't think just one thing will be the stand-alone to beat it. I'm fighting it on the medical front today, but I took a different tact last night.

I've read that the lung can be the place in our body where we might store or manifest our grief and loss. Have I had grief and loss over the last five years? Uh, yeah.

So last night I saw my long-time friend, Maureen, to help address that. She's a pastor and therapist, and very skilled as a spiritual director and leading people through healing prayer. I've seen her many times before.

What I'll say is that the session lasted nearly three hours, at one point I was sobbing, and I left feeling lighter. Done. Calm. Like I could "let it go."

Hopefully, my spirit is less "toxic," and the cancer won't be as happy in it.

February 29

I re-read this article I had published in Positive Thinking magazine a few years back, and like it even more now.

The Colors of Life

Don't settle for the imitations in life when you can have the real thing.

Its color caught my eye. The deep coral pink of each meticulously crafted petal. I'd been browsing in a gift shop when a bouquet of silk roses captured my attention. I reached to examine one with my fingers, running my thumb over the plastic beads that created a convincing replica of moist drops of dew.

I didn't buy the long-stem silk rose that day. But it did come to mind every now and again. I thought of it driving home from the hospital after visiting my friend of 20-plus years for what I knew would be the last time.

Before I even stepped into her hospital room that evening, I knew it wouldn't be good. We were just getting back into town the day after Thanksgiving, and I prepped my kids as best I could.

"Her body's really sick," I began. "It's fought for a long time to stay healthy, but it's giving up – it's wearing out." I told them about IVs and bandages, bruises and stitches from surgery. "But remember," I said, "inside she's still Lori."

And I was right – she didn't look good. A genetic miscue had left her waging a variety of physical battles since she'd been 12. And now, at 38, her armor had been stripped. I noticed her color – or lack of it. Her sallow skin was white and, in some places, seemed nearly clear, revealing bluish veins and burgundy blood vessels that had once been hidden.

Lori's vision was gone, but she could hear us that night and responded here and there.

I held her hand while I described our family feast the day before. I recounted our adventure of just two weeks prior, when she and I had frequented a favorite Chinese restaurant. Her then failing sight was limited in the ambient lighting, and I'd bumped her into a table. I read the menu to her before we decided on Moo Shu pork, chicken with broccoli and spring rolls.

The kids were getting restless in the crowded white room, so I reluctantly said my goodbye. "I love you, Lori." I squeezed her hand. She squeezed back. And then my children and I made our way back down the winding gray halls.

The drive home offered somber moments to talk about death. "She's going to die very soon, and when she does, her body will be all better – it won't hurt anymore."

After a moment of silence, my 7-year-old said, "At least there aren't any hospitals in heaven."

"No, Elisa, no hospitals in heaven," I replied.

Lori had experienced more than her share of hospital stays. But she was almost done. I smiled and cried thinking about her dancing and laughing – completely pain free. She'd be getting her color back very soon.

During the remainder of that quiet drive home, the image of the silk rose again crept into my mind. I wondered why I didn't buy it – a cheerful addition to some corner of my home, frozen in eternal bloom. It's tempting to buy imitations. They look perfect every day and their color never fades. But the dew is paralyzed on the leaves, and the odorless petals aren't as delicate as the real thing.

Fresh flowers are a lot of work – trimming the stems, pinching off extra greens and arranging them just so. They don't last long enough to collect dust.

But — they're alive. And with life arrives inconvenience, and also the rich colors and remarkable aromas that imprint our senses when we enter a room. Yes, they peak quickly, and then soon fade. Within days, their dried stems and wilting petals top the trash. Because with life comes death.

As headlights twinkled in my peripheral vision, I thought of all the living colors that penetrated my life: my relationships, my kids, and my faith. I thought of my children's eyes; one daughter with blue-green and the other with bright blue, and my son with dark hazel. I remembered the eye-popping purple lilacs in the spring and the vibrant brushstrokes of a recent sunset. All these snapshots captured in my mind, but all of them fleeting and ever-changing.

"These are the brilliant colors of life," I thought, "something imitations can only hint at – never match."

My friend, now gone, had color in her life – and she added it to the pallettes of everyone she knew. For her, and all of us, our lives ebb and flow, colors shift and fade. And although hers paled earlier than most, her memory reminds me of the importance of noticing – every day – the rich hues of life around me.

Of course it's easier not to look – it hurts less when they fade. But had I not walked with her, neither would I have the beautiful memories.

So now I try to look around more. I stop and stare. I let the colors of life catch my eye and give my gaze permission to settle for awhile. My heart is more tender, but my life more blessed and richer for the seeing.

Spring

March 2

Chi chi!

My house is full of gizmos — a hothouse, a chi machine and ERE machine. I'm not sure exactly what they all do, but I can say that since my November surgery, the back of my neck has been really stiff. After a week of "chi-ing," it's loosened up and doesn't hurt anymore.

For good or bad, the hothouse (far infrared light) puts me to sleep. I'm getting the kids on these things too, and on Friday night Matt was under the hothouse. He has a tough time calming himself down to get to sleep. That night he laid down, I left the room, and went downstairs. I'd forgotten to tell him something, so went back up, and he was out like a light. Wow. That never happens.

The next morning I said, "Matt, you fell asleep really fast last night. Maybe the hothouse helped." "Do you think I should try it on a school night?" he asked. "Absolutely!"

So we'll see. Obviously, these are all in the house because I'm hopeful they'll have some positive effects against cancer. So far, they don't seem to hurt.

March 4

Back on the cruise ship – chemo Round 2

I tried to predict my symptoms this round based on my vast experience from Round 1. The problem? The doctor increased the dosage, and effects are supposedly cumulative.

So on Day 3, the day I was knocked out last time, I laid on the couch for 10 hours. What a waste of a day. I did watch two movies though. Neither were great.

Yesterday, I figured all would be well for a big event I'd helped plan at work. A 50-year anniversary celebration marking the day when our company headquarters moved from its downtown Minneapolis office and eight miles west out into the boonies — namely Golden Valley. The office opened on March 3, 1958.

I didn't feel horrible, but got achy from standing and talking to people (which I love to do). After ramping up for it, I crashed right after. I got home and took a three-hour nap. OK, three-and-a-half hours.

Today I woke up a little woozy. I got all the wave action of a cruise ship, but none of the fun in the sun. I was perfectly fine as long as I didn't stand or move. Hence, I had a very prolific work writing day.

I feel OK now, and trust that I'll perk up tomorrow.

March 8

A word about Dan

Actually, more than a few words. There's a ton of you who haven't met him. So the next couple of entries will be about how we met.

Oh, and by the way. My name is still Suzy Goodsell. I didn't change it so I'd have the same last name as my school-age kids.

The story of Dan & Suzy

Back in 2005, I jumped into the curious world of match.com – an online dating service. Looking at the options that quickly appeared in my inbox, I put one to the side, thinking that he and I could hit it off.

But first, I responded to the extremes – the intense conversationalist and the salsa dancer. Interesting, but not my type. But then I had to respond to Dan. After all, he'd read "Lord of the Rings" several times before he saw the movies.

And we did hit it off.

We wrote – exchanged emails and holiday pleasantries. "Can we talk on the phone?" he asked, only several weeks after some intermittent exchanges. "Sure," I replied.

He sent his phone number, and without hesitation, I dialed it while I sat on the entrance ramp that prefaced my long commute home.

He was as quick in conversation as he'd been in written messages. His voice – friendly. And his laugh, warm. We talked about nothing and everything until I pulled into my garage, and even then, I lingered before disconnecting to enter my other life.

My other life. The world where "mom" was the operative word. Certainly not "adult woman." But another call followed, and a few late into the night. "I'd like to meet you. Maybe for coffee?" he said.

Making plans

We agreed on that Thursday — a nice place not far from either of us, and on my route home.

It had already been a tough day – attending the funeral for the mom of a friend of mine. Her mom had swiftly fought and lost the cancer battle. My friend – in her early 20s – was reeling from the loss and juggling a demanding law school schedule. The service was moving, and of course, I wept for her loss.

Then here I was – on my way to meet the words from my inbox, and voice from my phone. I guess I was lucky to meet someone at all. I'd shed more than one tear despairing over the improbability that I'd find anyone from my three main watering holes: home, car and work.

But I had. In just three weeks, I'd found several interesting online distractions. Engaging, but several were certainly not long-term potential. I was hopeful as I approached the restaurant, slowing for the final stoplights between me and Rockwoods Grill.

New thoughts crossed my mind. What if we hit it off? Where in my life is there any room for someone new? And how does someone new fit into the life that now is mine?

No time to ponder that one. My car stopped in an unexpectedly great parking spot. Without hesitation, I adjusted my scarf and stepped boldly into the lobby.

And so we meet...

He'd said he'd be wearing a cowboy hat. A cowboy hat? Was this so I could quickly identify him, or an important statement about his personality? Uh-oh. He hadn't mentioned "cowboy" on his profile.

Whatever the reason, he was easy to spot. I strode in and quickly saw him. He leaped up – a bit too quickly, making the bar stool waiver a bit. I extended my hand for a professional handshake, saying, "Hi, I'm Suzy." "I'm Dan – don't I even get a hug?" Well, OK.

We grabbed a table, one of the tall round ones. The initial chit chat about our day proved to be interesting fodder – a bit reflective right away, given I'd just been at a funeral. As it turned out, he'd also attended a funeral that day – a friend of his who had lost her daughter.

It seemed a bit incongruent – talking about loss with someone I'd just met. And yet, we hadn't just met – our words had darted back and forth, and so had our voices via the phone. But here we were — face to face.

And while disclosing my somber day, I also found myself inwardly assessing him. Polite enough. Cute. Feeling a bit nervous. But me too. Handsome – his eyes were happy. He was easy to read. And when he laughed, his whole face laughed, exuding joy right from his gut. Tall enough. A bit stout. But comfortable.

A minute later, 90 had passed. I was burning the candle on the other end with a babysitter at home, who I knew was eager to leave.

Weekend plans

Neither of us had kids during the upcoming weekend – and the movie "Narnia" was opening. Both of us were eager to see it. I wasn't sure my kids would be interested, and knew few of my friends would be. "We should go," I said. "OK."

He walked me to my car, through the deepening snow.

"Can I have a hug?" "I could get used to this." OK, that was a bit of a line – and I soon learned that this major movie watcher snatched more than a few one-liners to interject during poignant moments. "Who loves ya baby?"

Back to reality

On my way home, I reviewed our conversation in my head during the few miles I had left to go. Once home, the chaos of my "other" life consumed me.

"I have math homework!" "I need $5 for my field trip – I need the permission slip tomorrow!"

Although I typically collapse into a coma between the bed sheets by 9:30, I had one last thing to do.

I jumped online and emailed Dan. "Just so you don't have to worry – I had a great time tonight. I like you."

March 9

The very next night...

The time element didn't seem to be an issue those first few weeks. The night after we met in person, I planned to haul the kids downtown to a Christmas light parade. As we exchanged emails, he mentioned he worked downtown and I asked, "Why don't you join us?" I was going to be there anyway – and didn't immediately realize that he'd be meeting my kids AND my friends just 24 hours after our first face-to-face meeting. But what could it hurt? He was friendly enough.

It was a typically fast-paced event. Late leaving work, zooming home, wrangling the kids into snow gear and then into the car – then careening back downtown.

Oops

I forgot my directions. Always the planner, I'd "MapQuested" the route. But in my haste, I'd left the directions on the counter. Hmm. I called Dan. "Now how do I get there?" Within seconds, he had the directions for me. It'd be easiest to take 35-W to Washington. Then left on 2nd Street. "Still plan to meet me there?" "Absolutely."

I like this guy. After years with a directionally challenged spouse – he actually got maps. Kind of a turn-on.

This time, he slid comfortably into the crowd of kids and friends. We were scattered in the food court, trying to appease the diverse tastes. I quickly introduced him – as what, a new friend? I guess so.

I was distracted and felt like I couldn't pay much attention to him. After the dinner frenzy, we filed down to the street to claim spots on the curb. It was cold. Although milder than some Minnesota winter evenings. But still.

Dan's work pants were thinner than what he might have worn had we actually planned this. But I admired his spontaneity and courage, really, for joining this mob. The kids opted for the curb rather than the chairs I'd lugged down. But that gave Dan a spot by me, and an opportunity for me to share the comforter to help keep his legs warm.

Who is he???

The 20-minute parade was soon over, along with the oohs and aahs and Santa's finale. I found him terribly helpful in packing up all our gear, and as he loaded himself up like a pack mule, I felt grateful for the help. "I'll drive you back to your car." He directed me back to where he'd parked. After our quick goodbyes, he stepped out and shut the door. Elisa, my then 9-year-old immediately interrogated me. "Who is he exactly?"

"I just met him – last night actually. We'd emailed and talked on the phone. He's a friend."

That sated her – for the moment.

March 10

And finally...

> *"Stop searching forever – happiness is just next to you."* – Anonymous

That's what I realized about a year ago this time, after concerts, musicals, trips to Chicago, Duluth and Washington D.C. After lots of movies, laughing and fun. After weeding tomatoes and building a deck.

I'd wanted love in a lightning strike, but instead it rolled in slowly like the tide, creeping imperceptibly closer with each wave until it surprised me in its embrace.

I shouldn't have been shocked, I guess. The lightning, while exciting, had always burned me in the end. The electricity felt exhilarating but left me smoldering and alone. I didn't know love's approach could be so subtle. A slow warming versus a startling shock.

Whatever my expectation, it happened nonetheless. Though I can't say just when it crossed that invisible line, I finally stared at what was all around me and dared to call it what it was.

Still, my inner critic was skeptical. Just like how those who get saved in an instant, recalling the time and date, will "poo poo" the seekers who in their search for God realize a slow-ripened faith with no clear beginning. I get it now. They didn't recognize what they had because it felt different from what they expected it to be.

It was the same with me.

March 12

Lung draining

Checking to see whether or not there is fluid in my lung has been a very odd experience. After the tube had been inserted at the hospital, Dan and I watched an instructional video on how to perform the draining procedure at home.

There is about 12 inches of tubing inside me, and maybe eight inches poking out through a hole in my left side. The tube is coiled around and covered with a white adhesive patch.

During the next month, we only tried draining it four times. A few days after it was inserted, we drained out 275 ml of pale beer-colored liquid. A week later, we got 50 ml. Two weeks later, nothing came out at all. That's good!

Dr. Dan

Fortunately, Dan had paid attention to the instructional video, as this would have been uncomfortable doing it myself. First, he unrolled a new kit containing all the supplies, then he slipped on the surgical gloves that were included. He untaped the adhesive patch on my left side.

Next, he removed the clamp on my tube, and attached a tube connected to a pressurized plastic bottle, also from the kit.

When he removed the other clamp, the bottle created a vacuum, and it sucked air out of me!

Actually, the goal was to suck any accumulated lung fluid – but that only happened the first time.

What did it feel like? Similar to someone vacuuming out my insides. It didn't hurt really, but it felt very, very strange.

Next, Dan detached the bottle, rewound the tube on my skin, and covered my side with a brand new five-inch square patch. And – yahoo – it was done!

The whole time, Dan was very careful and precise. I was tempted to find him a surgical mask to complete the whole "doctor" look. But he did great, and I was happy that he was there to do it.

March 14

This morning's chest scan update

I had a high-contrast CT scan this morning. The doctor had left a message for me at work before I even got back to the office.

"Good news, overall," he said. I'd worried a bit, since he'd sounded so eager to talk to me on his message.

There was a marked decrease in fluid on my lung — very little fluid was present, in fact. My left lung is completely re-expanded (the lower half had been collapsed back on January 31). The big tumor has shrunk a bit after the first two chemo rounds: from 9 x 7.6 cm to 8.6 x 5.5 cm.

Of some concern are some large nodes on the lower left lung — but he thinks those were probably already there, just not visible through all the fluid. And there are scattered nodes on right lung — "slightly more prominent," he said.

He gave me the go-ahead to get this ridiculous tube out of my side. It had become increasingly uncomfortable. My side was sore off and on throughout the day, and it was impossible to sleep on my left side.

At least I didn't have to wait all weekend to hear the scan results. I'll see him at 9 a.m. Monday, then I have Round 3 of chemo two days later.

He said since I'm tolerating the present treatment, we'll just keep moving forward. I'd hoped for more shrinkage and even "disappear-age" on that right side...but it is overall improvement, so I'll take it

Thanks for your continued prayers and support.

March 19

All hooked up

I'm more than halfway finished with Round 3 at the clinic. My white blood cell count had been down when they drew blood two days ago, but today they leaped up. If they're too low, the doctor will postpone chemo.

I've been a bit down this week — maybe because of the low blood counts, or maybe because the doctor looked at me happily on Monday and said, "We can't cure this tumor, but we're going in the right direction."

Ick. I don't fault him for calling it what it is, but he reminded me that I have a life-threatening illness, and I'm not sure what to do with that. "The biology of the disease is different from the biology of the individual," and "The diagnosis does not determine the reality."

That's what I do with it.

But still, after only four-plus months, I'm already finding it hard to sit with that "diagnosis" every day. Denial is fun, but not helpful.

Plus, my eyebrows officially fell out last week, which adds to my evolving appearance and challenges my skills with a brush at a very early morning hour as I attempt to replace them.

March 22

Waiting day

Yesterday was Good Friday. Tomorrow is Easter. And today, we wait. Caught in the in between that is our life.

How awesome that you, Coco, signed the guestbook on my blog site just yesterday. I've been thinking about the very first entry in the "Journey into Rest" book, by Elizabeth Sherrill, that you gave me. I keep hanging there, reading it again, again, and can't seem to move on into the second reflection.

Abraham stepped into the unknown.

"Go from your country and your kindred and your father's house to the land that I will show you."
— Genesis 12:1

The author writes:

"God's marching orders to Abraham are the very ones He gives to you and me at the start of each year, each week, each day.

"Leave the past behind. Venture with Me into territory you have not yet glimpsed!

"Leave behind old hurts and hates, old limitations. And leave the good as well: last year's insight, the truth that was so stretching yesterday. Dare for the better. Abraham's kindred were not evil — they were simply not all that God had in mind for him.

"Where is God leading you now? You will only know by setting out. The direction was all God would show Abraham in the beginning, not the destination. The journey itself, the putting of one foot after the other in faith, is to be our great training ground in trust."

I've already set out. But I keep asking God where he is leading me. What I know is that my direction is forward, one foot at a time. I need to be content with that for now. And believe he's forging trust within me.

March 29

Cancer heroes

I feel fortunate not to have any friends or family members who have really battled cancer. My grandma, now 90, got breast cancer in her 80s, treated it and is still living.

Someone commented the other day that they couldn't believe I was making plans, just doing my life. What other alternative do I have? I haven't watched someone's journey to know how to "do" cancer treatment. She laughed and told me, "That's good!"

Those I have met are survivors, not really dealing with it now. Except for Sheila, who is living with it and treating it after nine years. In our brief conversations, she's been a terrific encouragement.

I guess the advantage is that my cancer heroes are much further down the road. I never saw them when they were at where I'm at, but want to someday be where they are. I get to chart my own course about how to "do" the journey in between. That's a good thing.

March 30

Quick request

I'm giving a talk tomorrow (Monday) at work from 1 p.m. to 2 p.m. I'm excited about it — but am worried a bit about coughing a lot. I'll be talking for 45 minutes, and would appreciate your prayers.

This is one of those incidents where I want to plan to do things, but want to be able to follow through with them.

March 31

I didn't cough. Even once. I shouldn't be surprised — but that's so cool. And (so far) rave reviews. Thanks all.

April 1

For those of you who asked, yesterday I gave a series of really fun vignettes from General Mills history for our "Newcomers Club" - folks who have worked at the company less than a year or so.

Starting in the 1940s, the General Mills Mechanical division had all sorts of government contracts and was well-known for being able to design and build precision equipment. Plus we were the largest toy manufacturer in the world in the 1980s! Imagine that.

I feel like the Cliff Clavin of the company.

April 6

Took a quick trip to Iowa on Friday and Saturday to visit my mom and dad, sister Lori, and my grandma Helen. Dan and I drove down to sunny, slightly warmer weather. It was 65 degrees or so yesterday. Today in Minnesota, it's upper 40s and RAIN. Dan and I had fun, too, driving down and back. Until I fell asleep on the way home for the last two hours of the trip. Then he entertained himself.

This has been people week. Ran into a high school friend, Anita, at the local Coffee Den by mom and dad's. Last Thursday, I had dinner with Diane from Colorado who was visiting her family in the Twin Cities. I figured out I've known her 25 years — since fall of freshman year at Bethel. At dinner, we laughed, cried, laughed, then cried.

Next week is busy too. First, the plan is to have my lung tube actually removed on Tuesday morning. They plan to use local anesthetic, but will still take it out in the operating room, just in case "yanking" it hurts too much. If it does, then they'll use the general anesthetic. There are 8 inches of tube on the inside, and 12 inches on the outside. Plus a 5"x5" dressing on my side. It's been there since January 31. Fun, fun.

Round 4 of chemo is in three days.

High school friend Susan will be in town the end of this week. I plan to connect with her for lunch on Friday before her 7:30 p.m. concert in Minneapolis.

One positive has been connecting and reconnecting with friends and family lately. It's been so great to have so many authentic conversations.

April 9

Three weeks go by fast

I'm hooked up the IV at the clinic right now for my fourth round of chemo. No new scans. Yesterday, I got the external tube removed from my side at the hospital.

I was in and out of the operating room in 20 minutes, and the actual "yanking" only lasted 20 seconds. But it was the longest 20 seconds ever. The alcohol swabs were cold and tickly — so I wiggled and laughed. Then they numbed it with a local: syringe-injected, you'll feel a "sting and burn." They did it four times. Once the doctor started clipping the stitches, I said "Ow!"

So they gave me another sting and burn.

It's hard to describe what it's like to have a 20-inch tube removed, some of which is slightly adhered to an internal organ. Pulling it didn't "sting and burn," per se, but was wildly uncomfortable.

I'm sure doctors and nurses prefer an unconscious patient so they can just do their jobs, rather than one who gives them all kinds of feedback, screeches and rolls around. But, having local anesthesia allowed me to get out of the hospital fast. But not without cost!

The good side is that it feels great now. Lately, it had been very achy from the friction whenever I was active or slept on it. So that's done.

April 10

Upcoming Benefit

Not knowing the future, my friends are wisely planning a benefit for my family. They've already contacted some of you. Thanks.

April 12

Busy week

After tube yanking and chemo this week, high school friend Susan was in town on Friday for her evening concert. Despite manic weather, she and I had lunch and did a flying tour around General Mills. Thanks for making the effort, Susan. After work, Dan and I went to her downtown concert. (www.susanwerner.com)

She's so talented. Remember, Susan, the night before I drove off to college? You sat by my bed playing guitar and singing until I fell asleep. A sweet memory.

Have I mentioned lately how grateful I am for the stellar people I have in my life? I really am.

Yesterday was a long day, though. Today, I'm a bit shot. Tired and achy. Luckily, no real plans. Tomorrow is another long one in St. Cloud with the girls' dance competition, but hopefully I'll recharge today for that.

April 19

Nothing to do

I've discovered that there's really nothing for me to do in the shower anymore. With chemo attacking the body's fast-growing cells, I have no hair to wash, and don't have to shave my legs or under my arms. So I scrub my head, wash all over and I'm done.

I'll stand under the warm running water just because it feels good. And to extend things out a bit.

This is why men take such short showers. I get it now.

Felt good all week. The only new annoying side effect is a constantly running nose and constant cough. Apparently, the chemo is hard on mucous membranes. Bleah.

April 20

Trade-off

So the time I save in the shower is now spent on applying my face. The Carboplatin/Taxol chemo mix successfully dropped my eyebrows. Now my eyelashes are thinned and random.

This results in the need for early-morning artwork. Eyeliner works pretty well for faux-lashes. But eyebrows are tricky. First, I can't really remember where they were. At home in Iowa, my mom gave me a few pointers, pulling from her experience when she daily drew on her mom's while she was caring for her.

If I get them on right on the first try, meaning even, level, not "surprised looking," then yahoo. Otherwise I can always erase. The trick is not to rub them during the day. I've alerted my women colleagues that I want them to tell me should I rub one off, or, heaven forbid, just rub the center of one off.

I want to know!

Fortunately, when my brimmed hats are pulled down, most eyebrow imperfections are shadowed a bit.

They promised "bright and 70 degrees" for this afternoon. It's now 42 and cloudy. I'm not feelin' it.

April 24

Happy Birthday!

Today Suzy is 44 (finally, an even number again). Send her joy-filled Happy Birthday thoughts and wishes. — Dan

April 26

Spring in Minnesota

After sunny and 70+ degrees just two days ago, this morning there is an overnight dusting of snow, and it seems to actually be snowing right now.

Thanks to all of you for the birthday wishes! Even though it poured rain all day and was freezing outside, it was a fun day. Dan and I went to Q.Cumbers (a buffet-style salad restaurant I like) and to Comedy Sportz, a comedy club in Minneapolis. That, combined with some YouTube video about the Hawaii Chair, and I laughed a lot.

I've been feeling fine – and after nearly six months, am generally tired of having cancer. I'm ready to move on. It's discouraging not being able to chalk it all up to experience and just get on with things.

April 27

ZZZZzzzzzz...

I slept a lot today. After getting a good night's sleep. Took the kids out to eat, to church then to see "Godspell" at the high school. Elisa found a hat for me that was 97 percent off – a $20 hat for 60 cents. She was so proud of it – it's perfect for sleeping. Soft and warm. Red and a bit "cat in the hat" like – but I love it.

Dan put together a basketball hoop and stand for Matt today. It took a bit longer than he anticipated, but Matt's very happy.

I think I slept today because I could. I seem to gear up for the week, but then need some evening naps and a weekend "slug" day. That was today.

April 30

Fun-filled weekend

I'm so grateful to those of you who are planning to come to the benefit on Saturday. I must admit, I'm a bit glad for the gloomy, cold forecast — it would be difficult to compete with our first 75 degrees and sunny spring day.

May 4

A word of thanks

There's one person who I haven't said enough about. And that's Dan – my husband of three-plus months. Without him, this path could have taken some very different turns. His love, support and presence has made a huge difference in this journey.

He's been at every appointment, scan and chemo. He's been my advocate and gets me to the right place at the right time for the downtown appointments. He knows how to navigate both the skyway and the tunnel systems at the University of Minnesota to find doctors' offices.

He's spent hours on the Internet doing research to figure out what the best supplements are for me to be taking — which ones are backed by research versus the ones that are just hype.

What would I have done without him in my life? I can't imagine.

So, Dan, thank you. I love you. I appreciate every day that you've walked with me and look forward to many more days of walking together.

May 6

Good news

I met with my oncologist this afternoon after all my scans. The main tumor in my lung shrunk from 8.5 x 5.5 cm down to 7.6 x 3.5 cm since the scan in mid-March. By our math, that's 40 percent smaller more than six weeks ago.

There are a lot of little tumors scattered on both sides of my lungs — but they've either stayed the same, or slightly decreased in size. They used the phrase "partially cavitated," which seems good, like they've got little holes in them.

The impression: Decrease in size in the large confluent mass. (That was the summary.) And nothing has changed from my brain MRI.

So, we'll do Round 5 of chemo tomorrow. Dan thinks that Dr. M was genuinely surprised by the results. I'm feeling OK, the tumors are responding, and my kidneys are doing great. In fact, they're functioning at 135 percent, and Dr. M always has to re-key in my numbers because the computer thinks he made a typo. "Are you sure?" it asks him.

The only concern this time is that my white and red blood cell counts are a bit on the low side. But the brain MRI showed congestion in my sinuses - I might have a sinus infection. As a precaution, I'm starting on an antibiotic today.

Thanks for your continued prayers — things are headed in the right direction. I, of course, wanted him to look at me and say, "We're not sure where the cancer went."

But I'll take this report for now!

May 9

The benefit

Our event last weekend was awesome. If you weren't there, I know you're eager to hear about it. I'm not sure of the exact attendance, but the turnout was great!

It was overwhelming to see how many came, gave or participated in some way. Wow. My daughter, Katlynn, even pulled two of her friends together to dance to their lyrical competition song from "Against All Odds." Perfect.

My mom and sister were up from Iowa. Saw lots of friends. It was a good day.

May 11

Hated the new shot

I got a shot of Neulasta on my way home from work on the day after chemo last week. I've heard it can knock you flat — for me, I was achy and "not right" Friday, and on Saturday, I felt really out of it. Very headachy and a little sick. The shot boosts the body's white blood cell production. Apparently, my body does not like to be encouraged in this way.

Today I feel really good. It's Mother's Day, and in spite of a suspect forecast, it's bright and sunny out. Maybe Dan can figure out one more supplement to help boost my white blood cell count naturally so I can avoid the shot next round.

I got the final numbers from last week's benefit. I'm humbled. It all will be tucked safely in my benefit account and offers a cushion for later, if needed, for treatment or expenses.

I can't believe the generosity of so many of you. Even Andrea, who organized the event along with Cassie, commented that it "exceeded my expectations." Thank you everyone!

May 21

Achy side

After a weeklong side ache, I went in to see my doctor yesterday. What started as an ache with every cough, built into what if feels like when you run and get a side ache. It happened whenever I moved around.

Concerned about fluid or collapse in my lungs again or a blood clot, I got another CT scan. The doctor leaped into the room after: "It's nothing! And the main little tumor on your right side is smaller!" I love his enthusiasm.

I have multiple tiny tumors on my right lung. Since the last CT scan only 12 days ago, the biggest one went from 9mm to 7mm. More of them were "cavitated," and there were no new ones.

"But why does my side hurt?" I asked. He said, "I can't believe it — after such good news!"

Well, he's still not sure why my side hurts. Maybe coughing has put stress on the tender areas where the tube and scope went in between my ribs. So, like any good doctor, he wrote a prescription: muscle relaxants.

What's this going to do? I have no idea, but took one last night and one this morning.

The school year is winding down, dance for the girls is done, and Katlynn's soccer has begun.

May 26

Memorial Day

Elisa's birthday was yesterday, along with my dad's. She turned 12, and Katlynn will be 14 on Friday, May 30.

The days and weeks are flying by. I'm gearing up for chemo Round 6 next week. After that, we may do one or two doses more since it seems to be working and not making me sick.

We had a wild weather day yesterday — humid and overcast until 3:45 p.m. and then the sirens went off. A "Doppler-indicated tornado." We never got a tornado here (some places did), but we got hail. Up to quarter size and a few nicks in our siding. Three hours later the sky was blue.

Peculiar fuzz

I seem to be growing white fuzz on either side of my head. The weird thing is that I have a teardrop-shaped patch of dark hair growing on the back of my head that's twice as long as the fuzz.

I asked one of the nurses last week if she'd seen a lot of people's hair grow back. She said that she had, but then I showed her the patch.

"Unique. I've never seen anything like that."

Great.

Actually, I didn't think hair even tried to come back until you'd been off treatment for two months. Apparently I have headstrong and unusual hair.

May 28

Angel hugs?

Perfect strangers greet me to send their well wishes. Over the weekend a woman in the grocery store parking lot said, "Excuse me, ma'am? Can I give you a hug?" "Sure," I said. So she gave me a big hug and whispered, "God bless you."

A woman at a restaurant approached me at my table, looked me straight in the eye and said with earnest, "You're going to make it. I'm a five-year breast cancer survivor."

Dan just disclosed to me (maybe since it's been six months since my diagnosis) that the very first doctor I saw last November (a neurologist) told him I had three to six months. Granted, he thought I also had other areas affected with tumors, but I just flew by the six-month milestone. Praise God for that one, eh?

Keep the prayers comin'!

I'm at chemo Round 6 today. Even though the doctor had prescribed another shot to bump up my white blood cell production — I said no way. Via phone, he laughed, and said that would be fine. My white blood cell count was fine this time, so no need. But even if I was borderline, I wasn't going to take it again.

Summer

June 1

Just got back

Spent the weekend at a retreat center just 30 minutes from home — Pacem in Terris — (pah'-chum en terrace, for those of you who like to pronounce words correctly) — it means "Peace on Earth" in Latin.

Run by staff in the Catholic tradition, it's an awesome place to get away. I used to go regularly, but was amazed to discover that it's been nearly five years since my last visit.

So it was just me and the clouds of just-hatched mosquitoes.

They have hats and mosquito nets in the cabins for those who want to enjoy the walking paths, lake and open air despite the vicious beasts. After watching hoards of them fling themselves into the huge cabin window trying to get in, I was not too proud to don the net.

God used the mosquitoes to teach me a good lesson.

Frustrated that another hermit had already grabbed "my dock," I went up the path a bit to find a bench. I completely wrapped myself in the net — except for my feet and ankle (I was wearing jeans, shoes and socks).

I kept trying to relax and enjoy the lake view, but couldn't ignore the pesky things buzzing around the net by my face. They couldn't get to me — they just bugged me!

I was so focused on the close-in annoyances, that I couldn't pause to take in the larger view. What I sensed is that I have many "bugs" in my life — those things — both large and small — that I try to swat at on a daily basis. But my frenzy keeps me from laying back and seeing the panorama before me — God's big picture. A breathtaking view.

I brought that lesson home with me.

And, by the way, when I did get out to the dock, I had a dozen mosquito bites on my ankles and above, where they crawled up the inside of my pant leg.

June 5

To set the record straight...

My ankles were covered. Shoes, socks and jeans. The mosquitoes landed on my socks and either got me right there or crawled up my pant leg above my sock. Evil varmints.

Another lesson

I brought something else besides mosquito bites home from the weekend. Feeling more tired than usual after chemo a few days before, I slept a lot. I was a little discouraged that I didn't spend more time praying, writing or just sitting with God. What sunk in was that God can meet me in my rest. Even in my sleep.

And I came home really refreshed. I think he was happy that I'd carved out the time to go meet with him.

June 8

16 x girls x 12 years old

We had a birthday party for Elisa at our house on Saturday for 16 of her friends.

We did a cool scavenger hunt that took a LONG time and everything was terrific for four hours during the activity, awards, presents and cake. But the party was five hours long. Oh well, live and learn. They had fun.

Also recently spent some more time with my prayer warrior Maureen, and two of her reinforcements, Kelly and Ann. These are anointed women, and I count myself blessed that they chose to invest that time in me.

Three hours long. Lots of talking. Lots of praying. Lots of affirmation. It was amazing.

One more step on my healing journey.

June 13

The road less traveled

> *"There is no quick-and-easy path to emotional health and physical well-being. Every (one's) emotional healing is different, with unexpected developments, down times, and joyous spurts of catharsis and insight.*
>
> *"In fact, if the road isn't bumpy, you might be heading in the wrong direction."*

So writes Alice Domar, PhD, in "Healing Mind, Healthy Woman."

This is highly encouraging for me. What it says is to run full bore into growth. There may be some bruises along the way — but do what it takes to confront emotional baggage. In doing so, optimal living is possible. And, I believe, optimal healing.

June 27

Redirect

I don't want it anymore. Cancer I mean. I want to give it back.

I got a CT scan a week ago, and met with Dr. M earlier this week. He was pleased with a minimal shrinkage of the main tumor and a handful of smaller ones.

After telling me a few weeks ago that he'd consulted with the "head guy" at the University of Minnesota, they'd decided it was OK to offer me a couple more rounds of the chemo I've already been on. In fact, I rearranged things this week to get on the schedule.

But my doctor had a big pow-wow with other oncologists at the University, and discussed my case (along with others) in light of some new studies.

Apparently, having six rounds versus eight rounds didn't impact survival rates at all. The extra treatments could be effective, but because they're potent drugs, he didn't feel good about giving me more if it wouldn't have a long-term impact. He said he could keep it in the quiver for later.

Next step

So, then what? He said there's been some promising research using a targeted drug called Tarceva. It finds the cancer cells and kills them, without doing so much other systemic damage.

I watched several videos about it on tarceva.com. It's a pill that you take every day. The side effects might include diarrhea and acne.

My platelets were low, apparently from having six rounds of chemo. So if we decide to use this, he'll wait until next week and give my body a brief rest.

Based on his meeting, the textbook treatment would be to take me off of all chemo, then rescan me every two months until the cancer started spreading again. At that point, he'd start a second line treatment. But he said, "With you, it's OK to throw away the textbook. Why wait for things to progress?"

I like him. He's on my side and very committed to keeping up to date on the latest research. He laid out three options. We can pick.

I was strangely sad after the appointment. Second-line treatment feels like I really have this and it's not going away. Dan and I were sort of comfortable with our chemo day routine – packing sandwiches and fruit and sitting in easy chairs with our laptops, working online with Wi-Fi. It was familiar. I knew what to expect.

Now a new drug. What's this one going to be like? I know it doesn't attack hair, so that's a plus. I guess we'll see.

July 7

This was a great weekend

I started taking Tarceva last Thursday. So far so good, meaning I haven't noticed any strange side effects. I take it at least two hours after eating and then need to wait to eat for another hour. The point? Take on an empty stomach and without food. I'll stay on it for six weeks and then get rescanned.

My hair — if you can call it that — is really taking off. The sides of my head are covered in black and mostly white fuzz. There are a few show-off hairs that are an inch long, but I can count them on one hand. I still have my mysterious black teardrop patch on the back of my head that is twice as long as anywhere else. No doctor or nurse to date has ever seen anything like it.

With this male-pattern baldness of re-growth, there is still nothing to speak of on the top of my head. I did, however, spot a few stubbly pioneers this morning.

My sister, Lori, came up several days ago and is visiting from Manchester, Iowa. We were non-stop for the first two days, but things have slowed down. Went to Dan's cousin's lake house on the Fourth of July, and then watched the fireworks in Elk River and more via Dan on the driveway.

Lori and I have been out walking nearly every morning, and I've enjoyed getting outside, and good conversations.

And it's back to work tomorrow after a nice break.

Keep the prayers comin!

July 12

Berries, berries, berries

Dan thought it worth a mention that a week ago today, he and I, Lori, and all the kids roused early to go pick strawberries. In no time at all, we carried 56 pounds out of the patch.

Needless to say, the rest of the day was spent "processing." But over the weekend, we had strawberry shortcake, strawberry malts, and strawberry pie. Dan made 24 pints of strawberry jam and froze a ton of fresh berries.

He and I are going to Duluth today for a quick overnight getaway.

One-week Tarceva update: I'm noticing blemishes around my chin. Dr. M would be proud, I guess, because that means the drug is working.

But my hair keeps coming in. Elisa examined my eyebrows the other night and was all excited to see some whitish hair. But then she said, "Oh, Mom. You could use a wax."

"Old" friends

We ran into Tim and Sandy last night at Chipotle's restaurant in Elk River. They were on their way to their cabin. We were friends in the late 80s at Church of the Open Door. I also have fond memories of watching Pee Wee's Big Adventure with you, Sandy, and laughing hysterically.

So that's what we rented last night. It still makes me laugh!

July 15

Duluth weekend

Dan and I stole away for an overnight in Duluth last weekend. We left Saturday morning and came home Sunday. We had a blast! Our hotel was right in Canal Park along Lake Superior. They offered complimentary bikes, so we used them. They were hysterical retro-style beachcombers — mine was aqua, Dan's was white with blue and red striping.

We watched the barges come in and out of the harbor, toured an ore ship and retired Coast Guard boat, and took a scenic train ride up the coast. We were only there for 28 hours, but it was a fun getaway.

Oh, and there was a pool on the roof of our hotel that was heated to 101 degrees. Pretty fun considering the partly cloudy and very windy weather.

And now back to work and reality. Still doing well on the Tarceva — except my face is breaking out more, which is very annoying.

July 19

Ahhhh!

It's so quiet. Dan took Matt and Seth to a "Dude's campout" yesterday with church. They'll return later this afternoon. Elisa left yesterday for a middle school adventure weekend with her friend's church, and won't be back until Sunday night. And Katlynn has been at the fair with her friends. She's here now, but is sleeping and won't wake up for a few more hours. Then, I'm sure, she'll be off somewhere again.

I actually watched TV last night — a rare occurrence — after our county fair parade.

Tarceva-taking is uneventful. Other than blemishes around my nose and chin, there are no other effects that I can tell. I hope it's doing its thing: finding the cancer cells and destroying them. It's frustrating waging a battle I that I can't see.

My eyebrows are coming back, although very light-colored, as well as eyelashes. I actually have used mascara for three days in a row. Rather than a receding hairline, mine is just the opposite, with more and more hairs appearing. It's like they're scaling up my head, creeping higher every day.

I'm more and more grateful for how I flew through radiation and those six chemo rounds. I keep hearing from others how sick they were from just one or both.

Why me?

Why did I skate through? No idea. Another unanswerable question, like "Why did I get this in the first place?" Maybe I've done well so far through a combination of many unnoticeable little things. I just planned to feel well. I kept active. I have reasons to get up in the morning. I'm taking LOTS of supplements. Sleeping more. I'm still using my hothouse. Plus, several hundred people are praying for me.

I'm sobered because I know things could change on a dime with one scan, but am grateful that eight months after getting the "C" diagnosis, I feel good and am still moving ahead.

July 26

Morning thoughts

Just got back from a walk, and have been thinking. I'm reading "Happiness in a Storm," by Wendy Schlessel Harpham, M.D., a doctor who received her cancer diagnosis in 1994.

Some of her ideas are intriguing:

> *You can feel healthy and get on with your life while your medical problems are being managed with therapy.*

> *...the development of effective treatments has made cancer one of the most curable of chronic diseases.*

> *Over 1 million Americans are now estimated to be living with cancer as a chronic disease.*

It's outdated to think of cure as the only way to physical healing... What does modern-day physical healing mean to you?

"For me," says the author, "healing is when my body is controlling the growth and spread of my diseased cells." She continues, "Some effective treatments won't cure you, yet may get your disease into remission or partial remission, or may stabilize or compensate for the abnormalities for long periods of time, thus allowing you to live a long and healthy life."

In my mind, it was all or nothing. All the cancer cells had to be eradicated or I was doomed. But yet this doctor had her first diagnosis 14 years ago, and several recurrences of unrelated cancers since.

But she just keeps living her life. She has treatments when the need arises, and keeps planning and living through it all.

Medically, living and thriving with cancer is a greater probability for me than a complete "cure." I'm doing that now! Of course, I still would like it gone — through divine intervention, which can mean God making it go away, or him stoking up the processes he designed (enhancing my body's natural healing efforts with boosts from medical science, exercise and nutrition).

Either way, the target for "success" just got a whole lot wider!

July 29

Sniff, sniff ...

Dan and I went to an appointment with my oncologist, Dr. M, today for a check-in after four weeks on Tarceva. Everything's going great. After hearing me complain about my face breaking out, he was a little tentative to add more drugs to my system just to help clear my skin. I kind of felt the same way, but wanted him to know that this is an annoying side effect.

After talking for a bit, he broke the news to us that he's moving. Family reasons. Because it's a much smaller city, he won't even have as cool of a job as he does here.

We're so sad. I love his optimism and straight-forwardness. He's totally committed to research and can quote trials and statistics for anything we ask about. Or, in rare cases, he's honest enough to say, "I don't know."

He leaves Sept. 15, so I'll still have one more appointment with him after my late August scans.

I admit, I feel a bit abandoned. Since January, we've spent more than a few hours talking to him. He's the one who caught it when my lung was half filled with fluid. And I get a kick out of how he and his supervisor think I have superhuman kidney function. I have no idea what that means, but he's always amazed by it.

So, along the lines of everything happening for a reason, maybe he's taken us this far, and my next oncologist will be just right for the next steps. We'll miss him though.

August 2

The exodus

Dan and Seth left for the Boundary Waters Canoe Area last week.

Now I'm packing up the Matt and Elisa to attend Camp Jornada — a camp designed for kids who have cancer, or have a sibling or parent with cancer. We're leaving tomorrow.

Katlynn isn't going. Long story. But rather than force her, Shaun (the kids' dad) offered to have her stay at his house so I can go ahead with all my "empty house" plans. I appreciated that.

Tomorrow when I drop off the kids at the camp near Rochester, Minn., my sister Lori and her new beau, Mick, are going to meet us there. They happen to be in Rochester for his family get-together, so I'll get a chance to meet him.

Went on two long walks yesterday and today. On the treadmill, I read. But it's nice to walk outside, look around, think and enjoy the fresh early morning air.

I'm looking forward to the empty house next week.

August 12

A blur

The house is filled up again, and last week was a blur. I never even got home before 7 or 8 p.m. each night ... too busy catching up with friends. Did I really think I'd stay home and clean? For a split second, but then I just made plans.

Dan and Seth survived the Boundary Waters — even when a bear paid an evening visit to their campsite and ate food from a "bear-resistant" barrel someone had purchased for the trip.

Matt and Elisa liked Camp Jornada.

Eight is enough

Now we're all gearing up for a weeklong RV camping trip. Dan's "Routhe family reunion" is Saturday, so we're headed down to Redwood Falls, Minn., on Friday with all four kids plus two of their friends.

On Sunday, we're meeting neighbors Bonnie and Monte at a camp ground and waterpark in Warrens, Wis., for a four-day adventure. All told, we'll have four adults and 10 kids in adjacent campsites.

We're telling ourselves that because each kid will have a friend, they will annoy each other less. We'll just keep telling ourselves that, and it will be all good. Right?

I continue to feel like my old self and decided that I could, indeed, "live with cancer" as long as I felt like this every day.

My next scans are Aug. 28 — that will be after eight weeks of taking Tarceva. I'll meet with the doctor after Labor Day.

August 14

Phew!

Why is it so much work to pack up and go someplace to kick back and relax? At 10 p.m. tonight, Dan and I were grocery shopping at Cub with Katlynn and her friend, mindful that we needed to pick up Elisa from a birthday party — also at 10 p.m.

Dan's still going to run errands now, and I'm going to bed. Since energy definitely peaks earlier in the day, I'll be up at the crack of dawn packing, checking our food list twice and not forgetting the kids' chore chart for the week. With 20 extra hands around, we're putting the kids to work.

Oh, and I've got work to do for my job in the morning as well, which actually is more peaceful than all the running around I'll do before and after.

I'm hoping that tomorrow at this time finds me snoozing peacefully.

We'll see.

August 22

Rollin', rollin', rollin' ...

We're back. After starting out five hours later than planned last Friday, we arrived in Redwood Falls, Minn, for Dan's "Routhe Family Reunion." It's the 45th annual one they've had in a row.

But the trip wasn't without its moments. We were driving a 1984 RV. That says a lot, right there. Above the driver's seat and front passenger sheet, there was a handy storage shelf where we stashed all the bedding. As we ambled down the highway, the shelf slowly lowered onto his head. My memory is of him pushing it back up every few minutes. I suggested he alternate arms for a more balanced workout. He didn't respond.

But he had it fixed by Sunday, when we headed to the campground in Wisconsin. Met the Howerton's en route on exit 45 on the interstate when they had some axle trouble on their trailer. In two hours, Monte made several trips to Fleet Farm and cobbled together a fix that lasted exactly the 90 remaining miles we needed to go ...

August 24

Smarter than the average bear

This park is a bit of a throwback to the 50s. The Yogi Bear show was launched in 1958, and was one of the most popular cartoons in TV's early years. It continued in various forms until the 1990s, but I'm sure none of my kids had seen even one episode — until this week. At the park, they showed several episodes at 9:15 p.m. every night until the 10 p.m. movie started. The moon was full while we were there, and it was so perfect watching movies outside until midnight with bright moonlight, no wind, comfortable temps and no bugs (I'm sure they sprayed the grounds).

Having a friend for each kid was definitely a good idea. Along with our neighbors, we slept four in each camper and had six kids outside in three tents. And did I mention that we had perfect weather? Cloudless blue skies and 80s all week. Wednesday morning was a bit overcast, but it cleared up by noon.

It was ideal in that we'd all congregate around breakfast and dinner — but the kids paired off and went their separate ways all day — indoor and outdoor water parks, a beach, swimming pools, slides, and mini-golf. Katlynn and her friend, Taylor (both are 14) spent most of their time taking showers and "getting ready." For what I'm not sure, but they did spend a lot of time walking around, which apparently requires a lot of prep work.

August 26

More jelly stuff

One day the boys played dodge ball. Dan and I were going to play the Newlywed Game, but we didn't get dinner made in time. But he was adventurous and entered the "My Dad's Better than Your Dad" competition. Seth and I were there, and then Katlynn and her friend, witnesses to his fifth place finish (out of 10).

In each round, dads competed to "not be last." So in the jump rope competition, the first one who missed was out. Other contests were based on audience applause.

Dan survived hula hooping, jumping rope, an original cheer, the "I'm a Little Teapot" re-enactment (which included singing the song), and even the push-ups.

What got him? The Yogi Bear impersonation, which I thought he did pretty well.

He was a good sport.

We got home Thursday, just in time for Katlynn to get to her high school orientation. And rounding out the week, we all went on Friday (except Katlynn) to see the "Star Wars: Where Science Meets Imagination" exhibit at the Science Museum of Minnesota. As a fan, it was very cool to see all the models, miniatures and movie props.

What's next?

Now we're planning the summer's last adventure: canoeing and tubing in northeast Iowa over Labor Day weekend.

September 1

Laboring on Labor Day

Last Friday, Dan and I and the four kids headed south to meet up with my sister, Lori, the man she's been seeing — Mick — and his kids and other friends. We camped just west of Decorah, near Bluffton, Iowa.

Appropriately named, it was gorgeous. Some canoed and others floated on tubes down a section of the Upper Iowa River. It was lined with lush trees and big white limestone bluffs cut through by glaciers, and now the river.

The weather? Amazingly perfect. Again. Not sure when my weather luck will run out, but we've had a terrific August. It was great to see Lori, and have Dan meet Mick and their friends. The kids — all 16 — connected right away, and had a blast.

Came home last night and was glad to have a day to recover today — and do laundry. I accidentally washed and dried Seth's cell phone. So if anyone has a working Verizon phone that's not being used, he may be in the market...

Dan spent the day at his farm installing a wood laminate floor in his hallway and extra bedroom. I spent a few more hours tackling our basement to prep for building two more bedrooms. I slowed down when I went through a box of high school and college memorabilia. I still couldn't throw any of it away.

Health update

I feel good. Sometimes I say that with a bit of trepidation, hoping there's never a time when I feel horrible, but wondering if there will be. I had my brain MRI and full body CT scan done last Thursday — and my follow-up doctor appointment is tomorrow to see how the Tarceva is working. It's always a bit unnerving going in — did it shrink, grow or stay the same?

I have no idea.

Fall

September 2

Happy dance

In doctor-ese: Dramatic decrease in size of left lung mass, satellite nodules and multiple right lung nodules.

Bottom line: Everything got smaller

Dr. M was so happy — he said they've had some patients who have had remarkable results on Tarceva. Clinically, the trials would say that those with the best outcomes fell into three categories: non-smokers, women and Asians.

Well, I've got two of the three, but Dan's convinced I must have some Japanese ancestor dating way back.

What is true is that the main tumor that measured 10 cm back in January has steadily decreased and is now 3.9 x 1.9 cm. All the "satellite lesions" around the main tumor "have resolved with residual scarring." After eight weeks on Tarceva, the main tumor went from 7.6 x 3.5 cm to 3.9 x 1.9 cm.

Nothing new

On the right side, everything previously seen "has resolved (dissolved) or decreased in size. The largest nodule in the right lung on the previous study now measures 3 mm in diameter compared to 8 mm in the previous study. No new lung nodule is identified."

Oddly, I apparently have a healing fracture on one of my lower left ribs. It must have happened sometime since May.

And even the tumor cavity in my brain is healing up nicely.

Well, the numbers say it all. Tarceva has been used for cancer patients since 2001, and was approved for lung cancer only two years ago. As long as it remains effective at shrinking tumors or keeping them at bay, it can be used long term. So I guess I'll take the skin breakouts for now — and who knows what drug will come along next.

I'm so grateful for the good news. To God, for medical technology, and for all of you.

And for Dr. M who thought "outside the box" and gave me Tarceva right away without waiting the standard three months after first-line chemo. Yahoo! Let's keep up the good work!

September 13

Another week...

It's been nearly two weeks since my great doctor news — and the days keep zooming by. I've been sharing the news with folks who don't read the updates. It still feels a bit odd sharing results that are only detectable with million-dollar equipment. I wish I could feel the cancer going away. For that matter, I wish I could have felt it coming on.

At church, Eric (the pastor) is talking about having friends "who watch your back." Your entourage. I feel I have that, before and now during this cancer experience, I have my own posse of people who are in my corner, silently praying for me and encouraging me daily. I know it because I can feel it.

Thank you. I notice.

One of the types of people he mentioned that we all need is a "rock." Though he fell into a couple other categories as well, Dan was the sole person I placed in this one. He continues to be the steady, grounding person in my life, walking with me on this journey day by day. I know he worries about treatments and upcoming scans, but at the moments when I need him, he's present and steadfast. Only later on do we talk about the scary moments.

Thank you. I notice.

And to everyone. God is so good. I plan to continue to pay it forward for a long, long time.

I'm not ready to say goodbye to summer yet, and already the first day of fall is approaching in a week. The kids are getting into the routine of school. I can't believe I've got a daughter in high school. When I grew up, ninth grade was still in junior high, so I keep picturing that as a ninth-grader, Katlynn's not that old — yet.

September 24

All's well that ends well
or when life gives you lemons...

Dan and I got tickets to the Vikings football game last Sunday. We brought along our neighbors and camping buddies, Bonnie and Monte, and a former babysitter, Katie (20) and her friend, Lindsay.

The seats were terrific. At the beginning of the second quarter, a 20-something guy staggered down and took an empty seat directly behind me. Five minutes later he "lost his lunch" all over my back! This included lots of beer and a newly eaten hot dog.

This was horrific, as you can imagine, and I was the only victim. Lucky me!

The stadium staff was tremendous, but it took awhile. I had to start at Fan Services, which was directly across the stadium from where the infraction occurred. A very long walk considering what was on the back of my shirt.

Once there, however, Lisa (bless her heart) helped me get cleaned up, washed out my jacket while I rinsed my T-shirt, and hooked me up with a new Vikings shirt. She put the newly rinsed shirt in a plastic bag and said she'd hold it for now, and deliver it to me at the end of the game.

It gets better

After some indecision, security finally put our group of six up in a private suite on the 50-yard-line, right behind the section we'd just been in. They brought in two plates of cookies, ice cream, and then stocked the fridge with cold pop and waters.

There was a TV with commentary in the suite, comfy chairs and it was much quieter than in the stadium seats.

Katie commented, "This is great! They're totally telling me what's happening in the game, I'm in a suite and we're eating ice cream. It's a bummer you had to get thrown up on, Suzy, but this is workin' for me!"

People have told me that when life hands me lemons, I make lemonade. After Sunday, my new twist on that is "When life throws up on you, at least you get to eat ice cream in the suite!"

PS: The Vikings won, 20 to 10. Unfortunately, Dan was disappointed that he missed the entire second and third quarters — right when the Vikings did all their scoring. :(

October 8

Expectations

I've never aspired to mediocrity. From a very young age, I expected more.

From a monologue called "Mighty Germ" that I delivered at a Brownie Girl Scout dad/daughter event, to the lead in a fourth-grade play. From reading at the chartreuse-color level when peers hung back in the primary colors, to having my first story – "The Green Ghost" — published in the National Weekly Reader when I was in third grade.

And that was elementary school.

Purple what?

Our church is launching a "Purple Cow" challenge to, among other things, live large. Rather than settle for average, God calls us to extraordinary living. Don't be the brown cow, there are plenty of those. Be purple – stand out.

That doesn't mean success how the world may define it, but rather constantly tuning in to God and how he designed us, and allowing him to use those gifts and the time he gives us to the fullest. To make a difference.

While I've always been purpose-driven, my cancer diagnosis and treatment rebooted my outlook on many things. I didn't expect to ever get cancer – and now I expect that I should feel good and improve. I'm on a good life path, but am I missing (or avoiding) a better or deeper one?

One thing I know is that leading writing groups and workshops energizes me and fills me up.

But I'm not sure this is the right time to start – we have so much kid running to do each night that I treasure the one evening I don't have to do anything. Right now, I'm not sure I want to give that up.

What's next?

The last time I met with Maureen, my spiritually-wise friend, she challenged me to pray this prayer: "God, what next?" I've been praying it off and on all summer, but want to hit it with renewed fervor.

"God, how should I spend my free hours, whether they're measured in decades, years or cups of coffee? What's the best thing I can be doing for you, right now?"

Is it having a heart-to-heart conversation with Katlynn? A date with Dan? A hot bath? Writing? Or time in prayer? There's no wrong answer, but what's the best one?

Please pray this with me — for me, and for you. And then we'll see what God accomplishes through us.

October 12

Three incidentals

I got a haircut. OK, a trim really with electric clippers. Well, just on the nape of my neck. Matt was in for his "before-school-picture hair cut," and I asked Sue to trim me up a bit. She asked if she could trim the spot on the back of my head (she said "tail"). It was 1-1/2" long, while nowhere else is nearly that long. Now it's a bit more even.

According to Elisa, my "floppy arms" are gone. We joined the YMCA that just opened .9 miles from our house, and, after nearly a year, I started doing weights again. I had been doing yoga once a week this summer, which is really the reason, since I've only gone to the Y for two weeks. But no more "bat wings!"

I got invited to be on a panel for a work conference in two years. I don't know the details yet, but I'm tempted to say yes, for the sole reason to have plans two years out.

October 17

Wishful thinking and healthy hope

I've been wondering this week why cancer drug side effects are always bad. I mean with the millions of dollars of research that goes into them and their exorbitant costs, why can't they come up with meds that offer perks?

I'm watching my face and neck and what doctors say is a "rash," but really looks like acne to me.

Why can't a drug kill cancer cells AND clear up your skin, rather than make it worse? Or restore color to graying hair? Or how about increasing your bust size, giving you more energy and vibrant, sparkly eyes? That would make the whole treatment experience so much more pleasant.

But side effects happen that drug makers don't plan for or suspect. Just like results: recoveries happen that no one can explain.

And although my perfect drugs might be wishful thinking, I'm thankful that I'm justified in having healthy hope.

"Today's survivors of devastating disease or illness — and there are millions of them — are living proof that there is always hope."
— Wendy Harpham, "Happiness in a Storm"

The author goes on to say that somebody is going to land on the good side of statistics — it might as well be me.

And as long as I stay on the good side of statistics, maybe I'll also have an unexpected drug reaction that prompts me to clean the house.

October 20

Happy birthday, Dan!

October 21

Scans tomorrow

I can't believe it's been eight weeks — but Dan and I head off to the Maple Grove clinic tomorrow morning to check me in for labs at 9:45 a.m. What "labs" means, is the first of several times they'll try to find one of my teeny veins.

Then, my brain MRI followed by the CT scan (X-ray) of the rest of me.

I won't know anything until next week when I have my doctor's appointment with my new oncologist – Dr. E. Some of the wait is by choice, so Dan and I can hear the report at the same time.

I wouldn't say I get anxious about the scans, but they are certainly on my mind. But thank you, Sheila, today for sharing the pre-scan phrase you live by — "the scans will give you the information you need to help you decide what to do next."

Thanks for your continued prayers and support.

October 24

Prick a little, talk a little …

Remember the song that was background to "Goodnight Ladies" in the musical, "The Music Man?" Its variation tells the tale of my scanning event:

Prick a little, talk a little,
Prick a little, talk a little,
Prick, prick, prick, stab a lot, make it really sore...

After labs were done (stab No.1), it took 45 more minutes, three techs, and five tries to successfully start the spot for inserting the scan dye. First they wrapped my arms in warm blankets, and then I held my forearms under warm running water. After folding myself in half and dangling my arms over the arm of the chair, she finally got the IV going. It's a good thing I'm back into yoga.

For the first time, we'd actually been early to an appointment, but we still got out of there late. :(

I know everyone's hopeful about the results I'll get next Wednesday. I am, but also am a bit guarded. I'm trying to distance myself a bit and just think, "It is what it is."

It's a good thing that God is bigger than all of this.

October 29

There is no mass

Great news this morning at the doctor's office. This just in from last week's scans:

"There is no residual distinctly identifiable left infrahilar mass."

This describes the site we've been tracking since my diagnosis last November which, at that time, was 10 cm. Last time it was about 2 cm x 4 cm, but now it is sufficiently dissolved and broken up to the point that there is no mass!

On my right lung, there are still eight or so small spots (2 mm - 5 mm), and those are unchanged since the last scan. The good news also is that "there are no new lung nodules," and there is significant improvement in my lower left lobe.

My brain MRI is virtually identical to September's, with a bit more healing evident. Sweet!

My new doctor, Dr. E, was pleased that I'm doing "remarkably well" on Tarceva. The plan is to keep on taking it daily for two more months, and rescan the first of the year.

Impatient patient

Dan is way happier than I am. While incredibly thankful to God and grateful for the prayers surrounding me, I'm still waiting for everything to evaporate. He reminded me that it took cancer several years to develop; it might take more than nine months of treatment to dissipate.

OK, so I'm more of a short-term project person than long-term. I'm ready to check this off my list and move on, but I have the notion that God's got many more lessons for me in the midst of this.

Again, praise God and thanks to you all!

November 5

Anniversary month

One year ago today, I was sitting in a meeting with a group from Corporate Services trying to give them feedback on how to communicate with employees. It was the first day that I experienced "symptoms."

I couldn't get my thoughts out, or even complete a whole sentence. I felt so self-conscious and was sure everyone in the room wondered why I worked in Corporate Communications. I certainly was NOT communicating!

The walnut-sized tumor in my brain, that day either hemorrhaged or swelled enough to bump into my verbal center. What had been silently growing for up to a year, finally captured my attention.

More to come

This month will mark for me many of these memories, beginning today and ending with the one-year surgery anniversary to remove my brain tumor on November 26.

I'm sure you have anniversaries too — both good ones and difficult ones. As I walk through these memories, I recognize that we celebrate Thanksgiving this month. I'm so thankful for so much. I thank God for how he has walked with me — exemplified by the support and care I've received from my hubby, and all of you.

I'm thankful for my family, and my positive attitude, that so many of you mention. I'm confident that it's God-given.

I'm thankful to be a year out from the beginnings of all this — I certainly feel older and wiser as a result. Someday I hope to thankfully celebrate with you many anniversaries of being cancer free.

November 27

Thanksgiving

I spent last Thanksgiving with family, thankful to be with them and for a day off from the latest scans, but worried about the diagnosis that may come. The next day we heard the report: "never-smoker" lung cancer that had spread to my brain.

This year

It's now a year later, and my medical file has expanded to include surgery, radiation, hair loss, eight months of chemo, and countless procedures, including having a drainage tube inserted, then removed, from my lung.

As a "healthy" 44-year-old, I've trudged through the intense emotions that arrived as I tried to make sense of this illness.

This Thanksgiving my thankfulness looks different. I'm thankful for the hope I've carried with me on this difficult road. I'm thankful that I feel good, and can exercise, work full-time and generally continue to "do life." I'm thankful that my last scan showed the lung mass that eight months ago measured 10 cm, has all but disappeared.

I'm grateful to God for how he's walked with me every day — through the support and care I've received from my husband, family, work colleagues, friends, neighbors, and church family. And of course, for the encouragement and many notes from friends, close and far, via this site.

I'm thankful to be a year out from all of last year's beginnings. With the prayers and support of my "community of care," I plan to thankfully celebrate this Thanksgiving and hope to celebrate many more joy-filled anniversaries.

The turkey's in the oven — let the celebration begin!

November 29

Prayer request for Dan's mom

Please pray for Josie, Dan's 81-year-old mom. She's on her way to another hospital right now with what looks like severe pneumonia.

She and Tom (her husband, Dan's dad) had been in Texas for a couple weeks, but Josie wasn't feeling well, so they flew back early yesterday. Dan picked them up at the airport and headed right to their regional hospital. They admitted her, but she had a rough night, and she's being transferred to a much larger hospital in downtown Minneapolis.

I know that Dan and I, and his whole family would appreciate your prayers. Dan's dad has had a long, tough day yesterday with the air travel, and it looks like another long one.

Winter

December 2

Josie update

After a very uncertain weekend, Dan's mom (Josie) seems to be improving. She may be out of ICU later this week, but in the hospital for awhile.

December 24

Merry Christmas!

Wow, it's been a long time. The month has flown by. Dan has been down to Abbott Northwestern Hospital to visit his mom 26 out of the 27 days she's been hospitalized. He just headed down there again tonight and won't leave until 4 a.m. when he will be relieved by his brother, Greg. They weaned Josie off the respirator today and are hoping for the best.

My favorite day

Christmas Eve has always been my favorite day. The anticipation that was so overwhelming as a kid, has turned into a wish that today would never end, or at least go in slow motion. Tonight the house looks terrific, the presents are wrapped, and all is well.

The kids didn't want to sit down and read "Twas the Night Before Christmas," as we always have, but when I said that I did, Elisa found the book and read it to me while I was putting dishes away.

Christmas Eve represents to me the hope of what could be, while Christmas Day seems more a disappointment. Not in what gifts were exchanged, but just that it's over. Tonight there's still magic in the air ... the possibility of reindeer on the roof. Church tonight reminded us that it really is just about the birth of Jesus. Without him, there would be no reason to celebrate. There would be no hope.

This year he has been a very real hope to me. I read again this week that most stage IV lung cancer patients don't survive the first year. Lucky for me my hope isn't in doctors and wonder drugs. I'm glad to have them, but ultimately, the only hope I have is Jesus.

Happy Birthday to the newborn king. May you and your family celebrate his wonder.

December 27

Passing

Josephine Routhe, Dan's mom, passed away at 9:20 p.m. on Christmas Day, Dec. 25 — her favorite day. She made it clear that morning that after 28 days in the hospital, there would be no more tubes, no more pills, no medications and no respirator.

In the early 1900s, two brothers married two sisters and settled on adjacent farms in Redwood County in central Minnesota. One family had seven children, the other had 13, of which Josie was the youngest.

Her mother, also named Josephine, died giving birth to Josie in 1927, so Josie immediately went to live with her Aunt Kate and Uncle Pete next door. Josie didn't know that Kate wasn't her real mom until her First Communion.

Josie had fond memories of the weeklong Christmas celebrations she spent with her 19 cousins. And as an adult, her Christmases were also filled with family. The day's festivities were generally over at 9 p.m. or so — and Josie died at 9:20, somehow knowing that Christmas Day, for her family, was done.

So she went home. To finish celebrating in God's presence.

December 31

Say yes to the new year

Dan and I just came back from seeing Jim Carrey's latest movie — "Yes Man." On New Year's Eve, I typically will jot down a few thoughts about the past year, now slipping away, and set some goals for the next.

I remember writing a "post-dated" letter last year — I think I dated it one year in advance — probably Christmas or New Year's Eve 2008. I can't find it at the moment, but recall that I was celebrating a full year, a full life, and complete recovery. I always aim high.

It was hard to write those words, dated 12 months in the future, and believe they could be real. On Christmas Eve 2007, I laid awake "what-iffing."

What if we're waiting too long to treat the lung cancer (by doing the whole brain radiation first)?

What if this is my last Christmas?

What if I don't get to see my kids graduate?

How miserable will I feel this year?

Will I have memory loss in two years?

Will I be here in two years?

What if I can't finish the kids' photo albums?

What if I was supposed to do more with my life?

*What if it **is** my time?*

That night I asked God to show me the purpose in all this — to be a light though I felt surrounded by darkness. I asked God to be my light. "I need you," I pleaded. "I need to know I'm not alone."

"Every tear's a prayer," a friend had counseled me earlier in the month. And that night, I offered up many.

I found powerful words in Ephesians 3:20.

> *"Now glory be to God who by His mighty power at work within us is able to do far more than we would ever dare to ask or even dream of — infinitely beyond our highest prayers, desires, thoughts or hopes."*

And also "So let us come boldly to the very throne of God and stay there to receive his mercy and to find grace to help us in our times of need." (Hebrews 4:16)

I've come a long way since that moment last Christmas Eve, and have gotten many of the questions answered. I stayed very close to the throne, because I was afraid to let go. And I'm much more hopeful and confident about those answers that still seem misty, and more at ease with not knowing.

But a few things I know for sure. There was much wisdom in tonight's movie (although a few parts toppled the PG-13 rating). What I know is that I will continue saying "yes" to God, and "yes" to living life.

God bless you every day in the new year, and may you notice it each time he does.

Bibliography

Anderson, Greg. Cancer: 50 Essential Things to Do. New York: Plume, a division of Penguin Putnam, Inc., 1999.

Domar, Alice and Henry Dreher. Healing Mind, Healthy Woman. New York: Henry Holt & Company, 1996, p. 179.

Remen, Rachel Naomi. Kitchen Table Wisdom: Stories that Heal. New York: The Berkeley Publishing Group, a division of Penguin Putnam, Inc., 1996, p. 13.

Schlessel Harpham, Wendy. Happiness in a Storm. New York: W.W. Norton & Company, Inc., 2005, pp. 44-46, pp. 231-278 (p. 270).

Sherrill, Elizabeth. Journey into Rest. Material reprinted from Daily Guideposts 1978 – 1989. Minneapolis: Bethany House Publishers, 1990, pp. 16-17.

Siegel, Bernie S. Love, Medicine & Miracles. New York: Harper and Row Publishers, Inc., 1986. Reprinted in 1998, 2002.

Siegel, Bernie S. Peace, Love & Healing. New York: Harper and Row Publishers, Inc. 1989. Reissued in 1998, p. 2, 63.

About the author

Suzy Goodsell has led nearly 350 hours of writing groups and workshops to fan the flames of personal growth in others. Her articles have been published in magazines, including Personal Journaling, Positive Thinking and Vocational Biographies.

As a full-time business writer, she won a 2005 Award of Merit from the Minnesota Chapter of the International Association of Business Communications (IABC) for online feature articles.

A lifelong learner, she's attended numerous writing workshops, including the University of Iowa Summer Writing Festival.

For additional copies, email GoodsellGraphics@gmail.com